Investment Appraisal

To Valerie, Catherine, Judith and Elizabeth

The M & E Handbook Series

Investment Appraisal

G Mott

Freelance training consultant; formerly Principal Lecturer in Financial Management at Newcastle upon Tyne Polytechnic

Pitman Publishing
128 Long Acre, London WC2E 9AN

A Division of Longman Group UK Limited

First published in paperback by Pan Books Ltd 1982, 1987
Revised edition first published by Pitman Publishing 1989
Reprinted in this format 1991

British Library Cataloguing in Publication Data
Mott, Graham
Investment appraisal.–Rev ed
1. Capital investment. Decision making
I. Title
658, 1′52

ISBN 0 7121 1016 X

Founding Editor: P W D Redmond.

Printed and bound in Singapore

Contents

Preface

This book was written with two audiences in mind. First are the many business, accountancy and management students whose course syllabi demand a sound knowledge of this important topic, particularly those on DMS, CMS, MBA, BTEC National Higher courses and professional accountancy finals in financial management.

Secondly, are the practising managers who need a working knowledge of investment appraisal techniques to allow them to participate fully in team decisions and to communicate effectively with other managers.

The approach taken is to demonstrate the practical application of appraisal techniques by use of many illustrative examples throughout the text. Further case studies and examination questions are at the back.

The opportunity has also been taken in this revised edition to update the UK tax material, to incorporate one or two newer ideas – for example, portfolio theory – and to include a new chapter on cost-benefit analysis of larger public sector investments.

This text does not attempt to contribute to the academic debate permeating the whole area of appraisal, particularly relating to the topics of risk and the cost of capital. It does attempt to discuss and demonstrate widely agreed principles and practices of use to students and managers in their decision-making rôle.

However, one should never lose sight of the fact that decisions can only be made and implemented on projects that are suggested in the first instance. We should encourage innovation and initiative and judge managers by their track record on past investments as well as by the predicted outcome of their new investments.

Graham Mott
August 1989

Acknowledgements

I would like to thank the following professional bodies for permission to use samples of their past examination questions both in the text and in Appendix 6.

The relevant body for each question is denoted in brackets as indicated below. Any suggested solutions are my own and not those of the body concerned.

The Chartered Association of Certified Accountants (ACCA) and (Certified Diploma)
The Chartered Institute of Management Accountants (CIMA)
The Institute of Chartered Secretaries and Administrators (ICSA)

I would also like to thank my colleague Brian Day for permission to reproduce the microcomputer program in Appendix 5.

1 What is investment appraisal?

Purpose

Managers are involved in money-spending decisions either as initiators of projects, or as top management putting the final seal of approval on other managers' plans. For example, functional managers may identify profitable opportunities and direct their staff to investigate them more fully. Other staff may approach a functional manager with their own ideas for new investment.

An awareness of the factors influencing the profitability of such investments must help managers channel the firm's resources down more profitable paths. In many firms it is left to the accountant to pronounce a verdict on the viability of a proposed investment project. This presupposes not only that he is trained in appraisal techniques (which he usually is of course) but also that he fully understands the marketing, production and human aspects of such proposals.

Many arguments favour managers from the whole range of business functions being involved in this decision-making. If you are a manager, you should be aware of the factors that are relevant to a project's profitability. You need to be able to talk the same language as financial managers and accountants. Most of all, you must be able to identify and generate potentially profitable projects for your firms.

Before we look at the appraisal of individual projects we need to examine the context in which firms make capital available for a variety of types of investment, a topic which goes under the banner of 'capital budgeting'.

Capital budgeting

Because capital is not free, and in many firms is often scarce, managers have to take great care where they invest their firm's scarce resources. Before any selection of individual investments can take place, top management have to decide how much capital to make available for the coming year.

Due to the long-term nature of many projects, some of those started in the previous year may need further funds to complete them in the coming year. New projects will also be started. Top management will have to consider these needs and will also have to give serious thought to later years so that projects, once started, are not starved of funds before completion in a subsequent year.

1. Pool of finance. Very rarely do we think of one particular source of funds being used on one specific project. We tend to think of all the different sources contributing to a common pool from which all projects are financed as illustrated in Figure 1.1.

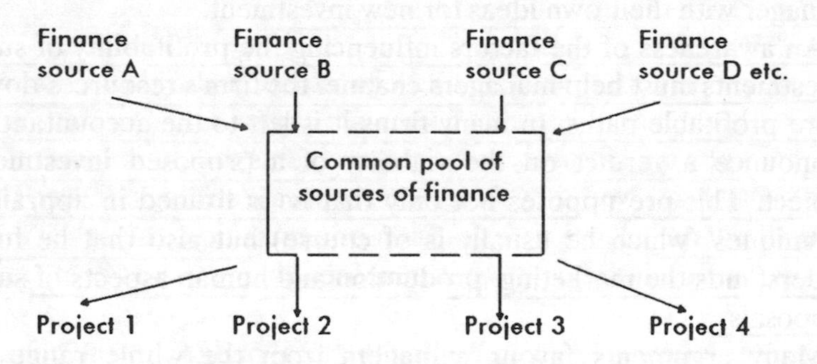

Figure 1.1 *The common pool of finance*

The reasoning here is that we should not accept one project financed from a cheap source, only to reject an identical project in the following month because it was financed from a different, but dearer source.

2. Sources of funds. Sources of funds contributing to the common pool for capital expenditure include:

(*a*) retained profit in the form of depreciation;
(*b*) other retained profit for the coming year;
(*c*) sale proceeds of surplus/redundant assets;
(*d*) grants/selective assistance;
(*e*) new loans;
(*f*) issue of new shares.

3. Types of projects. Investment projects themselves can also be classified, in this case according to their nature and purpose, as follows:

(*a*) legal requirements – to comply with health/safety regulations;
(*b*) replacement – the renewal of existing plant and vehicles;
(*c*) cost saving – the substitution of new equipment for less cost-effective methods;
(*d*) expansion – provisions of more working capital and/or fixed assets to increase sales volume of existing product lines;
(*e*) diversification – the introduction of new products requiring both working capital and fixed assets.

To some extent, a chicken-and-egg situation can now exist with top management not knowing how much capital to put into the pool without knowing the investment requirements of line management. This is partly answered by their own corporate strategy. If, say, they want to pursue growth by expansion or acquisition, then they must allocate sufficient funds for that purpose.

4. Capital budget. When compiling the total budget for the coming year, a useful way forward is to allocate funds to the above mentioned categories, or programme areas, before selecting the individual projects that can proceed.

EXAMPLE 1.1

X Ltd have budgeted a maximum of £770,000 funds available for capital investment in the coming year. Outline requests for authorisation amount to £870,000, being £100,000 more than the total budget. Top management decide to allocate the available funds as follows:

Investment category	*Amount requested* £	*Amount allocated* £	%
Legal/safety requirements	20,000	20,000	100.0
Replacement vehicles	100,000	80,000	80.0
Cost saving/efficiency	250,000	170,000	68.0
New products	500,000	500,000	100.0
Total	870,000	770,000	88.5

The implication of the budget in Example 1.1 is that top management agree that the company must meet its legal and safety obligations in full. They are also fully committed to implementing the new products, which are probably part of their corporate strategy. This means that the other two categories must be cut back as the total amount of capital requested exceeds the amount available.

Notwithstanding that regular replacement of vehicles is company policy, they are prepared to trim this category back this year in the light of other demands. The same observation applies to cost-saving investments where there is insufficient capital being made available to allow all viable projects to proceed.

Selection will be based on those which offer the maximum benefit for each pound invested, which forms the basis of the 'profitability index' calculation mentioned in a later chapter.

5. Project control. Once projects have been authorised, their progress needs careful monitoring, and each project manager should receive monthly reports on the costs incurred to date, analysed by element of cost and by stages of the project. A suitably designed job number, forming an integral part of the cost code structure, will facilitate this process.

EXAMPLE 1.2

If we take the four digit job number 8372, it can be thought of as comprising two elements. The digits 83 represent the job number allocated to a specific project whilst the digits 72 represent a particular stage or part of project number 83. If, say, there were 90 stages to project number 83 then they would be numbered 8301 through to 8390.

Top management also need updating on the state of the capital budget as a whole. They need to know how the total spent compares with the total budgeted for the year and, more particularly, how each individual project cost relates to the amount allocated. A suitable form of presentation for this purpose is shown in Fig 1.2.

The particular figures shown inform us that for project/stage number 8372 the total actual/projected expenditure of £25,800 exceeds the £23,000 originally authorised. The capital budget report will contain many such entries. Other stages of project number 83 will be adjacent to the sample entry illustrated and all other live projects in the current year will be included.

The totals of the vertical columns provide top management with vital information on the state of the capital budget as a whole. Total spending to date in the current year is disclosed in column 4. A comparison of columns 5 plus 6 with column 7 tells of the global over/underspend on all projects.

		Actual/projected costs				
1 Project number	2 Project title	3 Last year £	4 This year £	5 Total to date £	6 Additional to complete £	7 Authorised amount £
8372	New vent	5,200	9,600	15,800	10,000	23,000
8373	do	3,500	1,000	4,500	0	4,700
9101	New prod	0	7,000	7,000	83,000	90,000
9601	Cost save	0	8,400	8,400	0	8,400
	Totals	8,700	26,000	35,700	93,000	126,100

Figure 1.2 *Capital budget report*

Investment appraisal

The main purpose of this book is to look at the appraisal of individual investments, having recognised that this takes place in the context of an overall capital budget for the firm.

Investment appraisal is concerned with managers' decisions about whether, when and how to spend money on their firm's projects. Such decisions are important ones for the companies involved because often large sums of money are committed in an irreversible decision, with no certain knowledge of the size of future benefits.

EXAMPLE 1.3

Suppose a printing firm is considering buying a binding machine for £10,000 which will reduce labour costs on this activity by £3,000 every year for each of the five years the machine is expected to last. What the management of this firm have to consider – and this is no easy task – is whether a return of £3,000 every year for five years justifies the initial investment of £10,000.

The essence of all investment appraisals is to measure the worthwhileness of proposals to spend money, by comparing the benefits with the costs. If this measurement is done badly, it can hamper a firm's growth and employment prospects for years to come, and may lead to an inability to attract new investors.

Financial institutions and individuals provide firms with money in the expectation of a reasonable rate of return. If a firm invests that money in projects which do not yield a reasonable return then investors will be wary of that company in the future.

6. Cash flow models. We measure the worthwhileness of investment proposals by building simple financial models of the expected events.

EXAMPLE 1.4

Using the binding machine example above we can set out the expected events as cash inflows or outflows for each year of the machine's life. These cash flows start at Year 0 which is the beginning of the first year when the project is initiated. Cash outflows are denoted by a minus sign and cash inflows by a plus sign. We can see that the investment in the binding machine is expected to yield a profit of £5,000 in total over its five year life.

Financial model of the binding machine project:

Year	£
0	– 10,000
1	+ 3,000
2	+ 3,000
3	+ 3,000
4	+ 3,000
5	+ 3,000
Total profit	+ £5,000

The two main aims of this book are to identify the various items to include in the yearly cash flows and to examine the available techniques which say whether the investment is worthwhile or not. Subsequent chapters discuss the techniques in depth and show the build-up of the yearly cash flows allowing for taxation, uncertainty and inflation. But because no firm operates in a vacuum, so managers must also have an eye to environmental aspects.

Environmental aspects

When appraising projects, managers have to look at both the internal and external factors affected by their decision. If the proposal is, for example, a diversification away from existing activities, we must first see if it fits the corporate strategy laid down by the board of directors. The alternative is to question whether such investments warrant a change in that strategy.

Managers today are much more aware of their social responsibility to employees. How does the proposal under review affect present employment and future promotion prospects? Will the firm compete or even survive if it does not innovate?

Looking outside the firm, managers should be aware of their responsibilities to the local community in terms of the environment, pollution and employment opportunities. There are also the 'knock on' effects of services to be provided locally to the firm or to its employees.

Firms also have responsibilities to the nation. They contribute taxes to help finance centrally funded services. Their exports, or import substitutes, help pay for our importation of essential food and raw materials. Last but not least we must consider the needs of the customer, without whom the firm would no longer be in business.

All of these internal and external factors may influence investment decisions but these are outside the scope of this book, which primarily concentrates on the financial aspects of the decision. This is not to suggest that the financial factors are paramount, but that this book intends that managers should make investment decisions in the full knowledge of the likely financial consequences, not in ignorance of them.

We now need to look at the variety of situations which demand the manager's attention and require him to make good decisions.

Types of investment situation

There are a number of basic situations where an appraisal method assists a manager to make a sound decision. These include the following:

(*a*) Expansion – assessing the worthwhileness of expanding existing product lines requiring extra investment in buildings, plant, stocks, debtors, etc.;

(*b*) Diversification – assessing the viability of the more risky investment in totally new products;

(*c*) Cost saving – assessing the profitability of a cost saving scheme, e.g. when a machine replaces an existing manual process;

(*d*) Replacement – deciding whether and when to replace an old machine with a new one to save operating costs or reduce wastage;

(*e*) Alternative choice – deciding between alternative investments to achieve the same ends, e.g. when two mutually exclusive machines have different financial characteristics;

(*f*) Lease or buy – comparing the cost of purchasing an asset outright with the alternative cost of leasing.

All the above investment situations have the same common approach. In each case we must decide whether the benefits we get from the initial investment are sufficient to justify the initial capital outlay.

The next two chapters examine the available techniques used to decide whether an investment is worthwhile. Further chapters then explain how the yearly cash flows are built up in these investment situations and how the effects of taxation and inflation can be incorporated.

7. Non-quantifiable benefits. There may be some investment situations where no benefits are quantifiable in monetary terms. For example, the government may require firms to invest in fire detection and alarm systems in all their premises. In this case firms have no choice, and although there will be benefits in employee welfare, these are not readily quantifiable in cash terms.

Even in this situation an appraisal technique could be used to help us make the choice between competing systems which have different us make the choice between competing systems which have different financial characteristics. In the case of the fire detection and alarm system, one supplier's equipment may have a high capital cost but a low maintenance cost over a long life. An alternative supplier's equipment may have a low capital cost but high maintenance costs over a short life. We need to formalise this information to make a rational judgement as a later chapter on life-cycle costing demonstrates.

Risk and uncertainty

In most investment situations there is no certainty that the eventual outcome will be exactly as predicted at the time of the appraisal. For example, only in the case of a 'lease or buy' appraisal may we be certain of the size and duration of the cash flows, since these are usually expressed in a fixed price contract.

Even in this case we may be uncertain about the effects of inflation which may turn out to be at a higher or lower rate than expected, and which will affect the 'real cost' of the leasing payments. Unless we go back to managing by the seat of our pants we are faced with this problem of uncertain future cash flows whichever appraisal technique we use.

8. Risk techniques. There are some crude methods we can use to minimise the risks involved. These methods include rejecting all projects which do not recover the initial investment in a specified number of years or varying the required rate of return according to how risky we view the project.

More scientific methods can be used on important project appraisals where the capital to be spent is significant given the size of that particular company. For example, one approach maintains that it is not the individual project risk that matters but its effect on the overall portfolio's risk. Therefore, when we evaluate a risky project we need to correlate the individual project risk to that of the existing portfolio of investments it would join if accepted.

Another scientific method is to test the sensitivity of the return on the investment to inaccuracies, or variations, in any one item in the cash flow whilst holding the other items constant. Computers have an important contribution to make here when reiterative calculations are involved.

Yet another method is to draw a decision tree which shows diagrammatically the various stages of a sequential decision process. Alternative courses of action open to the firm are depicted as branches of a tree and are assigned probability factors according to the likelihood of their occurrence. The value of each possible outcome is calculated by multiplying the benefit by its probability. The highest profit (or least cost) tells us which course of action to select.

A more thorough analysis of risk and uncertainty and a discussion of these techniques are contained in a later chapter.

Inflation

There may be a tendency for managers to ignore inflation in investment appraisals because its far-reaching effects seem incapable of quantification in any systematic way. It can, however, be viewed as just another uncertainty on a project and incorporated in risk analysis.

The existence of inflation distorts the value of money itself which means the yearly cash flows are a mixture of £ chalk and £ cheese. We therefore need to distinguish between the real return on a project and its nominal or apparent return.

9. Real or nominal rate of return.

EXAMPLE 1.5

If we receive £100 annual interest on a £1,000 bank deposit our rate of return is 10 per cent. This represents a real return of 10 per cent if inflation is non-existent, but if inflation is also 10 per cent our real rate of return is nil. In this latter case all the interest received is used to keep the value of the capital intact although we have still received an apparent or nominal rate of return of 10 per cent.

Managers must bear in mind this difference between real and nominal returns when appraising projects. We need to clarify which value of money should be used in the yearly cash flows. We must also decide whether the firm's required rate of return is to be expressed in real or nominal terms. These matters are explored more fully later on in the book.

How much should a project earn?

Firms need to obtain capital for a number of reasons. They need money to buy or extend buildings, to acquire additional or replacement plant, and to increase the amount of working capital tied up in stocks and debtors when sales volume increases.

These items are called assets and are shown in the company financial statement – called a balance sheet – which lists all assets and the sources of capital with which they were bought. Figure 1.3 shows these items in a vertical balance sheet format.

		£000
Fixed assets		
Buildings, plant , equipment, vehicles and furniture		100
Current assets		
Stocks of materials, work-in-progress and goods	60	
Debtors (customers' debts)	40	
Cash and bank balances	10	
	110	
Less: *Current liabilities*		
Creditors (debts due to suppliers)	20	
Bank overdraft	10	
Tax and dividends due for payment next year	15	
	45	
Net current assets (i.e. working capital)		65
Total assets less current liabilities (i.e. capital employed)		165
financed by:		
Long-term liabilities		
Loans, deferred tax		50
Shareholders funds		
Share capital, retained profits		115
		165

Figure 1.3 *Typical company balance sheet*

If capital had no cost, most firms would be inundated with proposals to spend it on one project or another. It is not free because the providers of that capital expect a return from the company for the use of their capital. These providers are either the owners of the business or financial institutions lending on a long-term basis. In the balance sheet illustrated in Figure 1.3 they provided £165,000 of capital in total.

10. Cost of capital. Owners provide capital in two ways. They provide the company with the original share capital which may be increased every few years by a further issue of shares via a 'rights' issue. In addition, and more significant for an ongoing company, the owners allow the company to retain some of the profit each year rather than pay out all profits as dividends.

Whichever form the owners' investment takes, it is only invested in the company in the expectation of a financial reward. This may take the form of income from dividends, or through an increase in the value of the shares.

Another usual source of capital is for companies to borrow money for a number of years from financial institutions. In return they receive a fixed rate of interest each year and get gradual repayments or one total repayment of the loan on maturity. Such loans are alternatively called mortgages or debentures.

If we accept that capital is not free then firms are required to earn a rate of return on investments at least equal to the rewards that will satisfy the mix of owners and financial institutions. No project should voluntarily be undertaken that does not meet this required rate of return unless there are overriding non-financial factors to consider.

Some firms express the required rate of return as the current cost of short-term borrowing on overdraft. This has the merit of great simplicity but does not take into account the cost of capital from the other more important sources. It also glosses over the point that companies should not invest short-term funds in long-term projects.

The cost of capital is influenced by the particular mix of capital used, as well as by the cost of each component in that mix. We must also allow for the effects of both taxation and inflation which do not bear equally on the different types of capital. A thorough discussion of the cost of capital is contained in a later chapter. But first we turn to the appraisal methods themselves.

Progress test 1

1. What sources of finance make up the pool for new investment?
2. Explain the purposes of a monthly capital budget report.
3. Use your previous experience to think of examples to illustrate each type of investment situation.
4. 'As the future is always uncertain it is a waste of time producing financial models for appraisal purposes'. Discuss.
5. An investor receives a nominal rate of interest of 11% when the inflation rate is 6%. What real rate of return does the investor get?
6. 'The cost of owners' capital is free because there is no legal obligation to pay dividends'. Discuss.

2

Conventional appraisal methods

A prerequisite for looking at real investment situations is an understanding of the techniques available. This chapter explains the two main conventional methods used when appraising investment projects and comments on their strengths and weaknesses.

They are referred to as conventional as they have a much longer history than the appraisal methods based on discounting, even though the latter have been in use for thirty years.

Yearly cash flows

All appraisal methods require an estimate of the yearly cash flows attributable solely to the project under review. These cash flows are fully discussed in a later chapter but a working knowledge is required at this point to understand the basic techniques which follow.

Typically there will be an initial cash outflow on a project being the cash spent on the fixed assets like buildings, plant, vehicles, machinery and the like. If any of these items need replacing before the project ends, then a cash outflow will also occur in that later year.

Other cash outflows may occur through the firm building up stocks or giving credit to its customers. These working capital items will be cash outflows at the beginning of the project or at some subsequent date if increased in amount. At the end of a project the working capital is released and becomes a cash inflow at that time.

Cash inflows mainly occur from sales revenue less their wage and material costs. No deduction from such income is made for the use of the assets as their total cost has already been shown as a cash outflow at the outset. The accountant's notional charge for the use of these assets is called depreciation. This is not a cash expense but a notional charge for a part of the acquisition cost in each year's profit and loss account over the expected life. Depreciation is therefore irrelevant to cash flows unless one is trying to convert an accounting profit back to the underlying cash flow.

On cost-saving types of investment the cash inflow each year is the value of these savings, again without charging any depreciation. The cost of the investment will still be shown in full as a cash outflow at the time of acquisition. It is worth emphasising at this point that profits which accrue from cost-saving investments are just as valuable as profits from investments extending the firm's output.

At this stage all cash flows are expressed in money of Year 0 value and inflation is ignored. A later chapter describes the impact of inflation on projects and examines the techniques available to cope with it. Many of the other points mentioned so far are elaborated on and illustrated by examples in later chapters but first we need a review of the basic appraisal methods.

Payback method

Simplicity is the keynote of this investment appraisal method. Payback measures the number of years it is expected to take to recover the cost of the original investment. It is calculated by estimating the annual cash flows from the commencement of a project to the end of its useful life.

Initially the outflow will be negative, but, within a year or two from the start of most projects, positive cash flows will occur.

EXAMPLE 2.1

The directors of G Ltd set a maximum period of three years within which any investment must be paid back. They are proposing to invest £200,000 in a machine to save labour costs of £50,000 per year. The machine is expected to have a useful life of six years. Starting at the point of time when the investment is made called Year 0 (which is in effect the start of Year 1) then the annual cash flows at each year end can be set out and the payback period calculated. This is equal to four years in this case.

Calculation of the payback period

Year	Annual cash flow £	Cumulative cash flow £	
0	– 200,000	– 200,000	
1	+50,000	– 150,000	
2	+50,000	– 100,000	
3	+50,000	– 50,000	
4	+50,000	0	Payback completed
5	+50,000	+ 50,000	
6	+50,000	+ 100,000	

Example 2.1 is found to have a payback period of four years. This is then compared with the three-year criterion set by that particular firm which would result in this investment being rejected. The apparent simplicity of this method explains its appeal and why firms find it attractive.

A survey by Pike of investment practices in large companies in the 1980s showed that four fifths of the 149 respondents used the payback method.

1. Weaknesses of payback method. Whether this payback approach will always lead to sound investment decisions can perhaps best be examined with the help of another example comparing one project with another. If the firm relied solely on quickness of payback then in Example 2.2 Project B would be the one selected. The weaknesses of this appraisal method soon show when the two projects are examined more closely. Although payback is completed more quickly on Project B at three years this is very close to the end of its four-year life, whereas Project A goes on for two further years. One serious disadvantage of this method, therefore, is that any cash received after payback is completed is totally ignored.

EXAMPLE 2.2.

G Ltd have £180,000 to invest and are trying to choose between one project which returns £50,000 each year for six years, and another project which returns £60,000 each year but only for four years. The firm still requires payback within three years.

Comparison of two projects by the payback method

	Project A		Project B	
Year	Annual cash flow	Cumulative cash flow	Annual cash flow	Cumulative cash flow
	£	£	£	£
0	−180,000	− 180,000	−180,000	− 180,000
1	+ 50,000	− 130,000	+ 60,000	− 120,000
2	+ 50,000	− 80,000	+ 60,000	− 60,000
3	+ 50,000	− 30,000	+ 60,000	0
4	+ 50,000	+ 20,000	+ 60,000	+ 60,000
5	+ 50,000	+ 70,000	−	+ 60,000
6	+ 50,000	+ 120,000	−	+ 60,000

Payback $3\frac{3}{5}$ years — Payback 3 years

Another disadvantage is that no attempt is made to relate the cash earned on the investment to the amount actually invested. It may be that Project A is more profitable than Project B when looked at over its total life. It may also be that neither project is profitable enough to persuade the firm to invest in them.

The payback method does not attempt to measure this total profitability over the whole life of the investment and other methods have to be introduced to do this. However, payback is still used, either as an indicator of risk or where a quick cash inflow is paramount. If it is to play a part in decision-making then it is best used in conjunction with other methods.

Referring to the above-mentioned survey again, of the large proportion of companies using payback less than one half regarded it as the primary method of evaluation and used it in addition to other indicators.

A variation on the payback method, which overcomes the criticism that the time value of money is ignored, is the use of a discounted payback approach. This is illustrated in Chapter 3 after discussion of discounting techniques.

Rate of return method

The rate of return used to be the main method of investment appraisal as it purports to measure exactly what is required, namely, the annual profit as a percentage of the capital invested. Its popularity still is evidenced by the above survey which showed it to have been used as a primary method of evaluation by one third of the companies sampled and used in all ways by one half of the total.

Calculation of the average profit is performed by taking the total profits earned on the investment over the whole of its life and dividing by the expected life of the project in years. Total profit is the total cash inflows less the total cash outflows which automatically takes depreciation into account.

The average investment is normally regarded as half the original investment on the grounds that it will be wholly depreciated by the end of its useful life. This means that the most typical figure to represent a gradually reducing investment over the years is the average of its initial cost and its fully depreciated value of zero.

EXAMPLE 2.3

Simple Ltd use the rate of return method to appraise their new investments. They are considering three projects A, B and C which differ in investment cost, expected returns, and length of life as detailed below.

Calculation of the Rate of Return

Year	Project A	Project B	Project C
	£	£	£
0	– 200,000	– 240,000	– 240,000
1	+ 50,000	+ 100,000	+ 70,000
2	+ 50,000	+ 90,000	+ 80,000
3	+ 50,000	+ 80,000	+ 90,000
4	+ 50,000	+ 70,000	+ 100,000
5	+ 50,000	–	–
6	+ 50,000	–	–
Total profit	+ £ 100,000	+£ 100,000	+£ 100,000
Average profit	£16,666 pa	£25,000 pa	£25,000 pa
Average investment	£100,000	£120,000	£120,000
Rate of return	17% pa	21% pa	21% pa

2. Weaknesses of rate of return method. At first glance the rates of return on the three projects might suggest that Project A ranks inferior to the other two projects because the 17 per cent approximate return is less than the 21 per cent rate on both the others. Because the 17 per cent return applies for six years whereas the 21 per cent rate applies for only four years some further analysis will be needed before such a conclusion can be drawn. The rate of return method does not readily rank projects in their order of merit.

Turning now to Projects B and C it may initially appear that a manager will be indifferent between them as they have an identical rate of return of 21 per cent. A closer look at the timing of the cash flows shows that Project B has superior claims over Project C.

This is because cash is earned earlier on Project B and can be used to repay borrowings or be reinvested earlier, thereby saving interest and/or making more profit. The rate of return method does not take this timing into account in the calculations. It concentrates solely on averaging the total profits earned over the whole life of the project, irrespective of the years in which they are earned.

Soon it will become apparent that the average investment is a statistical illusion. One reason is that tax allowances or any grant benefits are not evenly spread throughout the life of an investment. Another reason is to do with the power of compound interest, which we take into account when calculating the true rate of return on an investment.

True rate of return

The profitability of an investment should be measured by the size of the profit earned on the capital invested. This is what the rate of return method attempts to do without perfect success. An ideal method will not rely on averages but will relate these two factors of profit and capital employed to each other in every individual year of the investment's life.

A useful analogy can be made with a building society mortgage. In this situation the borrower pays to the society a sum of money each year. Part of this sum is taken as interest to service the capital outstanding, leaving the remainder as a capital repayment to reduce the capital balance.

The profitability of the investment from the society's viewpoint can be measured by the rate of the interest payment, assuming that the yearly capital repayments have paid off all the mortgage.

Example 2.4 shows that the building society is getting a return of about 13 per cent on the mortgage balance outstanding year by year, and the repayment of all its capital over the six years. The small amount outstanding at the end of Year 6 is equivalent to less than another 0.1 per cent on the interest rate.

Essentially this investment earns a true rate of return of almost exactly 13 per cent. This is in sharp contrast to the average rate of return method discussed in the previous section when this same Project A was said to give a rate of return of 17 per cent. The effect of compound interest on the high reducing balance in the early years means that the true rate of return is less than the average rate of return. This is particularly true with high rates of return and with investments that have a long life.

EXAMPLE 2.4

A building society grants a mortgage of £200,000 to a firm, to be repaid in equal instalments over six years with interest on the reducing balance at 13 per cent.

Repayment of a £200,000 mortgage at 13% over 6 years

Year	*Annual cash flow* £	*Interest at 13%pa* £	*Capital repayment* £	*Capital outstanding* £
0	−200,000	–	–	200,000
1	+ 50,000	26,000	24,000	176,000
2	+ 50,000	22,880	27,120	148,880
3	+ 50,000	19,354	30,646	118,234
4	+ 50,000	15,370	34,630	83,604
5	+ 50,000	10,868	39,132	44,472
6	+ 50,000	5,781	44,219	253

Summary

So far we have examined two methods of investment appraisal. The payback method yields useful information about how quickly money is repaid by a project but is not helpful in measuring total profitability nor in choosing between competing projects.

The rate of return method contains dangerous inaccuracies in its method of calculation by use of an average profit and an average investment value. When the time value of money is taken into account by calculating interest payments, the true rate of return is seen to differ from the conventional rate of return.

The next chapter goes on to explain in detail how these interest calculations are built into investment appraisal methods.

Reference

Dr R. Pike, CIMA, 1982. *Capital Budgeting in the 1980s: A major survey of investment practices in large companies.*

Progress test 2

1. Why is depreciation added back to profit to determine the cash inflow?
2. Would the directors of G Ltd. accept or reject the project in Example 2.1 if their maximum payback criterion was 5 years?
3. What weakness in the payback method does the use of a discounted payback approach overcome?
4. Why should payback be supplemented by the use of other appraisal techniques?
5. Explain why the accounting rate of return does not accurately measure the true rate of return on an investment.

3

Discounted cash flow methods

When identifying, in the previous chapter, the true rate of return on the building society's mortgage to be 13 per cent, the calculations involved were somewhat laborious. A simpler method is used in practice based on the following principle of compound interest.

EXAMPLE 3.1
Suppose £1 was invested one year ago at interest of 10 per cent per annum. After one year the sum has grown to £1.10. If it was invested two years ago it would have grown to £1.21 with the first year's interest reinvested.

We can now look at an extract from a compound interest table showing the above examples.

The future value of £1 with compound interest at 10%

Year	£
0 (now)	1.000
1	1.100
2	1.210
3	1.331
4	1.464

Compound interest measures the future value of money invested some time in the past. It is equally possible to look at money in the reverse direction when it is called the present value of money receivable at a future point in time. This concept of present value is at the heart of all discounting approaches to investment appraisal.

Present value

The present value of a future sum of money is the equivalent sum now that would leave the recipient indifferent between the two amounts as to which to choose. The present value of £1 receivable in one year's time is that amount which if invested for one year would accumulate to £1 in one year's time.

EXAMPLE 3.2
Using a 10 per cent rate of interest, £1 receivable in one year's time has an equivalent value now of £0.909 because £0.909 invested for one year at 10 per cent will accumulate to £1. The figure 0.909 is known as a present value factor because it can be multiplied by any future sum of money to find its equivalent value at the present time.

The following is an extract from the present value table shown in Appendix 2 compared alongside the compound interest factors at the same rate of interest. The two figures are related in any one year in that one figure is the reciprocal of the other.

Year	*Present value of £1 allowing 10% interest*	*Future value of £1 receiving 10% interest*
0 (now)	1.000	1.000
1	.909	1.100
2	.826	1.210
3	.751	1.331
4	.683	1.464

If we take Year 4 as an illustration of the relationship between the two series of factors, then 1/1.464 equals 0.683.

1. Present value calculations. Returning now to the building society mortgage example at the end of the previous chapter, this was shown to have a true rate of profitability of 13 per cent. The calculation can now be repeated using the simpler present value approach.

To do this the cash flows are tabulated yearly and brought back (discounted) to their present value by the use of present value factors at the appropriate rate. In effect, interest is deducted for the waiting time involved. The remaining cash, after interest deductions, is therefore available to repay the original investment.

The profitability of the building society mortgage is measured by the maximum rate of interest which can be deducted, whilst leaving just enough cash to repay the investment. This rate of interest is the same 13 per cent as previously found, disregarding the small deficit which again is equivalent to less than 0.1 per cent on the interest rate.

EXAMPLE 3.3

Calculation of the rate of profitability of a £200,000 mortgage repayable over six years at £50,000 pa with interest at 13% using present value factors

Year	*Annual cash flow* £	*Present value factors at 13%*	*Present value* £
0	−200,000	1.000	− 200,000
1	+ 50,000	.885	+ 44,250
2	+ 50,000	.783	+ 39,150
3	+ 50,000	.693	+ 34,650
4	+ 50,000	.613	+ 30,650
5	+ 50,000	.543	+ 27,150
6	+ 50,000	.480	+ 24,000
			− £150

The effect of using present value (PV) factors on the future cash flows is to take compound interest off for the waiting time involved. If a higher rate of interest than 13 per cent was applied, then not all the capital would be repaid over the six-year life. If a lower rate of interest was used, the reduced interest payments would increase the size of the present values. This would result in the mortgage being repaid in less than the six years stipulated.

Both methods of calculating the true rate of return arrive at the same conclusion of 13 per cent, even though at first sight they do not appear related. That they are related can be seen by comparing the capital repayments of the first method with the reverse sequence of present value in the second method. Apart from rounding off differences they are the same.

This will always be the case in examples where the yearly cash flows are a constant sum. However, the discounting method is equally applicable when applied to a fluctuating stream of cash flows and will give correct results with any fluctuating pattern of cash flows.

Net present value (NPV) method

We now want to make the transition to an industrial setting. Managers in industry can use this discounting approach to assess the profitability of their investments. The expected cash flows on a proposed investment are set out year by year and brought to a present value by use of present value factors at the appropriate rate.

Positive present values are netted off against deficit present values to arrive at the 'net present value'. When this net figure is positive then a scheme is said to be viable because the stream of inflows is sufficient to pay the interest at the specified rate. Conversely, when the net present value is negative then the proposed investment is not viable.

EXAMPLE 3.4

The directors of Z Ltd are considering investing £150,000 in a press to make and sell an industrial fastener. Profits before charging any depreciation are expected to be £60,000 in each of the first four years falling to £40,000 in Year 5 and only £20,000 in Year 6. After this the press will be scrapped with no significant recovery value involved. Z Ltd have a cost of capital of 20 per cent which is used to appraise all their investments. The cash flows can be set out and multiplied by the present value factors at 20 per cent to demonstrate whether this project meets the 20 per cent required rate of return as follows:

Calculation of the net present value at 20%

Year	*Annual cash flow*	*PV factors at 20%*	*Present value*
	£		£
0	−150,000	1.000	− 150,000
1	+ 60,000	.833	+ 49,980
2	+ 60,000	.694	+ 41,640
3	+ 60,000	.579	+ 34,740
4	+ 60,000	.482	+ 28,920
5	+ 40,000	.402	+ 16,080
6	+ 20,000	.335	+ 6,700
		NPV	+£28,060

The net present value (NPV) surplus of £28,060 means that the rate of return is more than the 20 per cent rate of interest used. This is because the annual cash flows are big enough to allow more interest to be deducted and still repay the original investment. Now we turn to an extension of this approach which measures the rate of profitability on an investment.

Discounted cash flow (DCF) yield method

The NPV method assesses a project's viability when tested against the required rate of return of that particular company. This required rate of 20 per cent in the above example is often referred to as the cut-off rate, or criterion rate, and as a minimum will equate with the cost of capital for that firm.

2. Further trial rate. Sometimes managers want to know not only whether a project is viable, but what rate of return they can expect on a project. To answer this question the NPV method is taken a stage further. The annual cash flows are now discounted at a different trial rate of interest. Such trial rate is an educated guess but if the original net present value calculation resulted in a surplus net present value, then a higher rate rather than a lower rate will be chosen.

EXAMPLE 3.5

Returning to our previous example of the purchase of a press for £150,000 by Z Ltd we will now assume a trial rate of 30 per cent and discount the annual cash flows by present value factors at 30 per cent:

Calculation of the net present value at 30%

Year	*Annual cash flow*	*PV factors at 30%*	*Present value*
	£		£
0	−150,000	1.000	− 150,000
1	+ 60,000	.769	+ 46,140
2	+ 60,000	.592	+ 35,520
3	+ 60,000	.455	+ 27,300
4	+ 60,000	.350	+ 21,000
5	+ 40,000	.269	+ 10,760
6	+ 20,000	.207	+ 4,140
		NPV	− £5,140

As there is a deficit net present value of £5,140 the rate of return is less than 30 per cent. This is because too much interest has been deducted to allow all the capital to be repaid. We now conclude that the true rate of return lies somewhere in excess of 20 per cent but below 30 per cent.

3. Interest rate/NPV relationship. If instead of going to a trial rate of 30 per cent the annual cash flows had been repeatedly discounted at 1 per cent intervals from the 20 per cent required rate then the net present values would read as follows:

Net present values at increasing rates of interest

Rate of interest	*NPV*
%	£
20	+28,060
21	+24,220
22	+20,500
23	+16,860
24	+13,440
25	+10,080
26	+ 6,860
27	+ 3,620
28	+ 640
29	− 2,280
30	− 5,140

This shows that before the 30 per cent interest rate was reached a net present value of approximately zero was found at the 28 per cent rate of interest. This 28 per cent is the true rate of return and is referred to by accountants and managers as the 'discounted cash flow yield' or DCF yield. In other words the DCF yield is the solution rate of interest, which, when used to discount annual cash flows on a project, gives a NPV of approximately zero.

As in many aspects of accountancy there is another term which means the same thing as the term DCF yield. This other name tends to be used widely by economists from whose discipline this appraisal method evolved, and is alternatively called the 'internal rate of return' or IRR for short.

The survey mentioned in the previous chapter found that over half the companies sampled used the DCF yield method. It also found it to be the most favoured primary method of evaluation, much more so than the related NPV approach.

Interpolation

It would be a tedious task to adopt the above method of successive discounting at 1 per cent intervals but fortunately this is not required. The NPV calculations at 20 per cent and 30 per cent yielded a surplus of £28,060 and a deficit of £5,140 respectively. This provides sufficient information to estimate the DCF yield reasonably accurately by interpolation.

The interpolation shows:

$$20\% + \left\{ \frac{28{,}060}{28{,}060 + 5{,}140} \times (30\% - 20\%) \right\} = 28.5\%$$

Another interpolation method takes the form of a simple graph with the rate of interest on the vertical axis and the net present value on the horizontal axis as shown in Figure 3.1.

The NPVs from the trial at the company's required rate and the further guesstimate are then plotted against their respective interest rates and the two plots joined by a straight line. The DCF yield is where the straight line intersects the vertical axis at a zero NPV – in this case at about 28 per cent. Even when both plots turn out to be on the same side of the vertical axis, extrapolation will determine the approximate DCF yield.

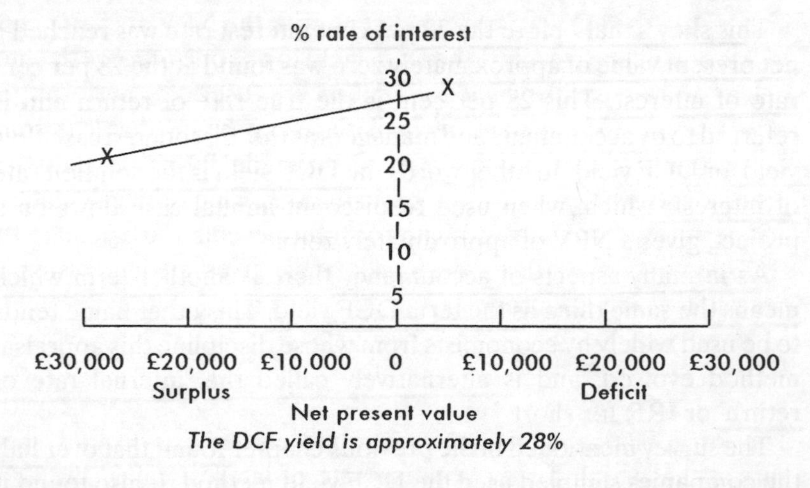

Figure 3.1 *Graphical interpolation to find the DCF yield*

4. Non-linearity. It may seem surprising that the relationship between the two points is shown as linear. This is approximately true although the line between two points is more curved when the rates of interest are in single figures. The exact line can be drawn on the graph by plotting all the intermediate NPVs shown earlier.

If the two plots are far removed from the actual rate of return the interpolation may not be quite accurate and it should be proved by a final calculation.

Calculation to prove that the DCF yield is 28%

Year	*Annual cash flow*	*PV factors at 28%*	*Present value*
	£		£
0	−150,000	1.000	− 150,000
1	+ 60,000	.781	+ 46,860
2	+ 60,000	.610	+ 36,600
3	+ 60,000	.477	+ 28,620
4	+ 60,000	.373	+ 22,380
5	+ 40,000	.291	+ 11,640
6	+ 20,000	.227	+ 4,540
		NPV	+ £640

The size of the DCF yield is 28 per cent to the nearest whole number. The surplus NPV of £640 is equivalent to another 0.2 per cent if we interpolate the NPV at, say 29 per cent, with the NPV at 28 per cent.

It is possible to calculate the DCF yield to use one or more decimal places, particularly when computers are used to perform the calculations. Although one decimal place may be justifiable in some cases, there is certainly no case to be made for more statistical precision. This is because the basic data on which the calculations are performed are only estimates of future events. To calculate the DCF yield to, say, three decimal places, gives an impression of precision which is illusory.

Other short cuts

The interpolation techniques described earlier are obvious short cuts in the search for the solution rate of interest called the DCF yield. Another approach is to use a microcomputer or programmable calculator to perform the interest calculations once the cash flows have been identified. A suitable program for use on a microcomputer will be found in Appendix 5. The use of dedicated programs or ordinary spreadsheets is particularly recommended to answer 'what-if' questions as discussed in a later chapter.

5. Cumulative PV factors. Another short cut is applicable where there is a constant annual cash flow in every year of a project's life. This method is based on the principle that if a constant cash flow is multiplied by individual PV factors, then the total present value will be the same as if the constant cash flow had been multiplied by the sum of the individual PV factors.

This principle is now illustrated:

(A) Calculation of the NPV using individual PV factors

	Annual cash flow £		*Individual PV factors at 25%*		*Present value* £
Year 1	+ 60,000	x	0.800	=	+ 48,000
2	+ 60,000	x	0.640	=	+ 38,400
3	+ 60,000	x	0.512	=	+ 30,720
			1.952		+£117,120

(B) Calculation of the NPV using a cumulative PV factor

	Annual cash flow £		*Cumulative PV factor at 25%*		*Present value* £
Years 1–3	+ 60,000	x	1.952	=	+£117,120

It can be seen that the NPV is identical on both methods but it must be stressed again that the cumulative PV approach can only be used where there is a constant annual cash flow from year one onwards. Year 0 is not included normally as very often the starting point of an investment is an initial cash outflow so it is a negative flow, whereas later cash flows may be the opposite sign.

Cumulative PV table. If the sum of the individual PV factors (1.952 in the above example) had to be arrived at by literally adding up the individual factors this might be thought to be a long short cut!

Fortunately a table exists with all the adding up done for the reader and the total of any number of individual year factors can be read off at a glance. Such a table is shown in Appendix 3 as the present value of £1 receivable annually, or put more simply, a cumulative present value table.

An abstract is shown below comparing such cumulative PV factors with the individual PV factors they represent. The cumulative PV factors are the sum of the individual PV factors except in the case of Year 5 when the third decimal place is slightly different. This is because the cumulative PV factors are calculated independently for greater accuracy rather than simply adding up the individual year factors. Hence it is possible to get rounding off differences.

Such differences have little practical significance, however, and the cumulation of individual factors can be safely used if a cumulative table is unavailable.

Relationship of individual with cumulative PV factors

Year	*Individual PV factors at 25%*	*Cumulative PV factors at 25%*
1	0.800	0.800
2	0.640	1.440
3	0.512	1.952
4	0.410	2.362
5	0.328	2.689

The main advantage in using a cumulative PV factor table is as a short cut means of calculating the NPV or DCF yield on a project. Because the cumulative table applies only to constant annual cash flows this techniques is usually used for rule of thumb calculations on a project's profitability.

Very often managers or industrial engineers want a quick guide as to whether it is profitable to pursue a certain course of action involving new investment. This can easily be done using a cumulative PV table when the cash flows are relatively constant. A more comprehensive evaluation incorporating taxation, working capital changes and inflation can be done later. The example overleaf illustrates this situation.

Example 3.6 shows how quickly the cumulative PV factor can calculate the NPV on a project with a constant annual cash flow from

Year 1 onwards. However, it can be used with even greater effect to find the DCF yield on a project with constant annual cash flows.

Here we require the cumulative PV factor to be first calculated and then looked up on the line of the relevant year of the cumulative PV table, in this case Year 6.

EXAMPLE 3.6

M Ltd are examining a proposal to introduce a fork-lift truck to handle palletised stock in a warehouse at a cost of £50,000. This can be expected to yield an annual saving in labour costs less truck running costs of £18,500. The vehicle and ancillary equipment are expected to last six years and the company regards a 25 per cent return before tax as a minimum requirement.

Calculation of the NPV on the fork-lift truck project

Year	*Annual cash flow*	*Cumulative PV factor at 25%*	*Present value*
	£		£
0	– 50,000	1.000	– 50,000
1–6	+18,500	2.951	+ 54,594
		NPV	+ £4,594

The project satisfies the criterion of a 25 per cent return before tax as a surplus NPV results when discounted at that rate.

Continuing with the fork-lift truck example the cumulative PV factor which gives an NPV of zero must be equal to £50,000/£18,500. This is the cost of the investment divided by the constant annual return to give the factor 2.703. This is virtually identical with 2.700, which is the cumulative factor for Year 6 at 29 per cent. The size of the DCF yield is therefore 29 per cent.

Comparison of appraisal methods

Four methods of investment appraisal have been discussed so far in these chapters – the two conventional methods of payback and rate of return, and two interest-based methods called net present value and discounted cash flow yield. Useful conclusions can be drawn by comparing these four methods when applied to the same projects as shown in Example 3.7.

EXAMPLE 3.7

Three projects A, B and C all have an initial investment cost of £200,000 but have different lives and different yearly cash inflows. These are set out below together with a summary of the appraisals by payback, rate of return, net present value and DCF yield methods.

Appraisal methods compared

lYear	Project A £	Project B £	Project C £
0	– 200,000	– 200,000	– 200,000
l	+ 20,000	+ 80,000	+ 60,000
2	+ 40,000	+ 60,000	+ 60,000
3	+ 60,000	+ 60,000	+ 60,000
4	+ 60,000	+ 40,000	+ 60,000
5	+ 60,000	–	+ 40,000
6	+ 68,000	–	+ 20,000
Total profit	+£108,000	+ £40,000	+ £100,000
Payback period (ranking BCA)	4.3yrs	3 years	3.3yrs
Rate of return (ranking ACB)	18%	10%	16.7%
NPV at 12% (ranking CAB)	– £884	– £12,580	+£15,100
DCF yield (ranking CAB)	12%	8.5%	15%

The payback method selects Project B as the most attractive investment but ignores the short life remaining after payback is completed. Even if Project A continued for 20 years it would be ignored by the payback criterion in favour of Project B. When the true rate of return, as measured by the DCF yield, takes the whole life into account then Project B is seen to be the least profitable of all three projects.

The conventional rate of return selects Project A as the most profitable simply because the average profit per year is more than in the other two projects. When the exact timing of those profits is taken into account then Project A is shown to give a DCF yield, or true return, of only 12 per cent compared with its rate of return of 18 per cent. Such inaccuracies in the method of calculation point to the rejection of rate of return as a suitable appraisal method.

Firms may sometimes calculate the rate of return expected in the first year of operation and compare this with the actual return earned in the first year for monitoring purposes. This monitoring or post-audit is an important part of capital budgeting and is discussed later. However, the complexities of taxation, grant assistance, working capital movements and other items further reduce the validity of the rate of return method.

A comparison of Project A with Project C on the DCF yield method illustrates that the extra £8,000 profit on Project A does not compensate for the slow build up of that project. With £8,000 less total profit, Project C is still more profitable than Project A because discounting emphasises the value of high earlier returns.

When the three projects are compared on the net present value method at a required rate of 12 per cent, only Project C satisfies that criterion. The three projects are ranked in the same order of preference as in the DCF yield method.

Ranking of projects

There are three methods we might use to rank projects that are appraised by discounting methods.

- By the size of their DCF yield.
- By the size of their NPV +/–.
- By the size of their 'profitability index' numbers on the NPV method.

These three ranking devices will not necessarily all rank projects in the same order as the section on capital rationing in Chapter 5 explains. Surprisingly, the NPV and its derivative profitability index turn out to be the main ranking devices. However, the DCF yield does play an important role in general screening.

6. Profitability index. The profitability index relates the NPV of all cash inflows to the NPV of the cash outflow on the project and is calculated by:

$$\text{Profitability index} = \frac{\text{NPV inflows}}{\text{NPV outflows}}$$

EXAMPLE 3.8
Taking Project C from the previous example as an illustration, the outflow was £200,000 and the NPV of the inflows was £215,100 (leaving an overall NPV of £15,100).

$$\text{The profitability index} = \frac{£215{,}100}{£200{,}000} = 1.075$$

Any project is viable when the index number exceeds 1.000 because this means that it is expected to earn more inflows, after deducting interest at the rate of its cost of capital, than its original cost. The relative profitability of projects can be measured by the size of their profitability index number. An alternative, and equally acceptable, way of calculating a profitability index number is to divide the NPV by the initial capital invested. In the case of Example 3.8 the index number would become 0.075.

Care must be taken when ranking in the two special situations of capital rationing and the choice between alternative or mutually exclusive projects. Certain rules apply in these situations and we return to this aspect in a later chapter.

Discounted payback method

Mention was made in the previous chapter that a variation of the payback method was to calculate the payback period on a discounted cash flow basis, rather than on the undiscounted cash flows. By this means, allowance is made for the time value of money. When payback is completed a firm will have recovered the cost of the original investment and allowed for interest for the waiting time.

EXAMPLE 3.9
Suppose a firm invests £200,000 in the expectation of earning £50,000 in each of the next seven years. Its cost of capital is 15 per cent. The payback period calculated on undiscounted cash flows is exactly four years, as it takes four lots of £50,000 to recover the original investment of £200,000. The discounted payback period is much longer, however, at nearly seven years. This is because the

present values used to repay the original investment are discounted at 15 per cent per annum. The time when payback is completed can be seen in the cumulative present value column below when the deficit turns to a plus in the seventh year:

Calculation of the discounted payback period

Year	*Annual cash flow* £	*PV factors at 15%*	*Present value* £	*Cumulative present value*
0	−200,000	1.000	−200,000	− 200,000
1	+ 50,000	.870	+ 43,500	− 156,500
2	+ 50,000	.756	+ 37,800	− 118,700
3	+ 50,000	.658	+ 32,900	− 85,800
4	+ 50,000	.572	+ 28,600	− 57,200
5	+ 50,000	.497	+ 24,850	− 32,350
6	+ 50,000	.432	+ 21,600	− 10,750
7	+ 50,000	.376	+ 18,800	+ 8,050
			NPV	+ £8,050

Summary

The profitability of an investment can best be measured by a technique which allows for the time value of money. This requires the use of either the net present value method or the discounted cash flow yield method, as both are based on interest calculations.

Which of these two methods to choose rests solely on the way the question is framed. If management want to know if a project reaches the minimum target figure, the NPV method will answer. If on the other hand, the size of the rate of profitability is needed, then the DCF yield will answer the question.

Both these methods bring each individual year's cash flow into account in the interest calculations, without resorting to averages. In this way they can adequately reflect the effects of taxation, asset renewal, inflation and other factors that cannot easily be incorporated in conventional appraisal methods like payback or rate of return.

Subsequent chapters now go on to describe how the yearly cash flows are built up and how we can incorporate these other factors in them.

Progress test 3

1. Compare and contrast the principle of present value with that of compound interest.
2. Recalculate the NPV in Example 3.4 using 15% PV factors. Explain why the NPV surplus has increased from the original £28,060 value.
3. Compare and contrast the NPV method with the DCF yield method of appraisal.
4. The NPV on a project is +£16,000 at 15% and +£6,000 at 20%. Find the DCF yield.
5. Use Appendix 3 to find the DCF yield on an investment of £100,000 that saves £20,000 operating costs each year over a life of 10 years.
6. Calculate the profitability index for the investment described in Example 3.9.

4

Determining the cash flow

The nature of any investment is the spending of money now in the expectation of getting money back in the future. No investment is worthwhile that does not recover the original sum invested and provide a reasonable return on the reducing capital outstanding year by year.

Cash inflows and outflows

Of necessity we must estimate and predict future events, irrespective of which appraisal method is used. These future events are depicted as either cash inflows or cash outflows to the business. We now need to determine precisely what they are in various investment decisions.

The chairman of a company usually comments on the financial affairs of his company in the annual report sent to its shareholders. 'Cash flow' is a term often used in this context and it refers to the profit from the trading operations that is to be retained in the business after providing for tax and dividend payments. To this retained profit is added the depreciation charge for the year to make up the cash flow.

1. Treatment of depreciation. It is not difficult to see that cash will be generated from the sale of goods or services after operating expenses are deducted. If there were no surplus cash there is no incentive to be in business. It is not so clear why depreciation should be added back to profit to determine the cash flow.

The reason why depreciation is singled out in this way is because depreciation is a notional item and not a cash expense. All other expenses charged against sales income are paid for in cash immediately or within the few weeks credit period allowed.

Cash goes out of the business at the time the asset is originally acquired, not when the company charges the profit and loss account with yearly depreciation over the expected life of the asset.

2. Profit and cash flow compared.

EXAMPLE 4.1

Suppose a company invests in plant costing £100,000 which it decides to depreciate at £25,000 p.a. over its four year life. Sales revenue amounts to £200,000 p.a. whilst operating costs amount to £150,000 p.a. When we compare the profit with the cash flow in each of the four years the following figures emerge.

Comparison of yearly profit with cash flow

Year	*Profit*		*Cash flow*	
0	–		– £100,000	
1	+ £25,000	(£200k–£150k–£25k)	+ £ 50,000	(£200k–£150k)
2	+ £25,000	– do–	+ £ 50,000	– do–
3	+ £25,000	– do–	+ £ 50,000	– do–
4	+ £25,000	– do–	+ £ 50,000	– do–
Total	+£100,000		+ £100,000	

In total the profit and cash flow are identical over the project's whole life, but the timing year by year is different. In essence the £100,000 cash outflow in Year 0 shown in the cash flow column is represented by the £25,000 p.a. depreciation deducted from sales revenue in Years 1–4 of the profit column.

This concept of the cash flow being the profit before charging depreciation, but after charging tax, is somewhat similar to the cash flows used in appraisal methods based on discounted cash flow. These cash flows take profit after tax but before charging depreciation, interest and dividends. The reason that cash flows are taken before interest and dividend deductions is that these two items are embraced by the interest rate used in the discounting process.

Apart from depreciation there are other reasons why the appraisal cash flows do not equate with the profit in the same year and these relate to the precise timing of the transactions. For example, a project can start at any time in a company accounting year and therefore Year 1 of an appraisal is unlikely to cover the same twelve months used for the company's annual accounts.

Also, the profit and loss account deducts the tax payable on the profit of the same year. In practice most tax is paid in the following accounting year and this later payment of tax must be fully recognised, as discussed in a subsequent chapter.

The final reason that cash flow differs from profit is that the whole concept of profit ignores the outlay, and recovery later, of working capital. The cash flows used in the discounting process take these into account, as and when they occur, in any year.

3. Working capital. Working capital is the amount of finance needed to prime the production/operation process by paying for labour, materials and other costs before the sale proceeds are recoved from the customer. The longer the production cycle and the greater the credit period taken by customers, then the more working capital will be needed.

Such working capital requirements never appear in a profit and loss account but are important cash flows in an appraisal of new products. By including working capital in the cash flows we take account of the fact that profit does not equate with the net cash inflow from sales. This is because of the credit received from suppliers, the credit granted to customers and the need to maintain stocks in many instances.

Fluctuations in such working capital items explain why the cash flow calculated from the profit plus depreciation was described as only approximate on an earlier page.

4. Types of cash flow. The best overall guideline to follow, when compiling cash flows for discounting purposes, is to place each item of the cash flows in the year the actual transaction takes place. In this way depreciation will be excluded, delays in making tax payments taken into account and working capital requirements shown.

The following list shows the most common types of cash flows to be included in an appraisal and may be useful when trying to determine which cash flows are relevant on any one project:

Checklist of types of cash flow

(*a*) Investment cost of replacement or additional fixed assets

(*b*) Opportunity cost of existing assets being recycled
(*c*) Workingcapital requirements, i.e. stocks, debtors less creditors
(*d*) Sales revenue
(*e*) Operating costs, e.g. labour, materials, fuel, maintenance
(*f*) Grants or selective assistance receivable
(*g*) Tax payments on profits
(*h*) Tax savings on allowances
(*i*) Scrap or resale value less disposal costs, if any

Timing of the cash flows

The conventional practice is to set out the relevant cash flows on a project on a yearly basis. The initial investment takes place at Year 0 which is in effect the start of Year 1. This may be the sole cash outflow or, as in the case of a large project with construction and commissioning phases, there may be negative cash flows for two or three years.

Subsequently the cash flows will turn positive as the benefits of the investment accrue. However, a negative cash flow can arise in any later year if a further investment/replacement exceeds the profit in that year. Typical patterns of cash flows may be:

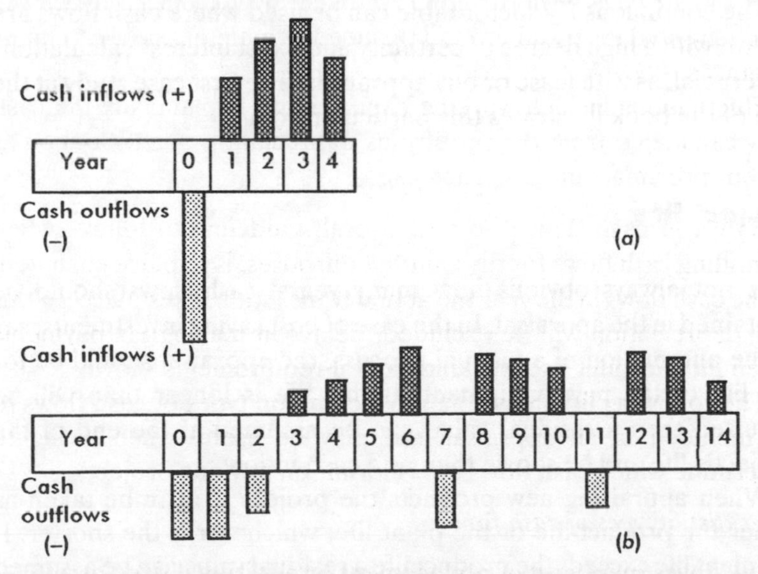

Figure 4.1 *Typical cash flow of (a) simple and (b) complex projects*

5. Discrete/continuous PV factors. The present value factors discussed in the previous chapter are used to bring future cash flows back to the same time value as at Year 0. By multiplying the future cash flow by a PV factor we are deducting interest for the waiting time. These PV factors are based on a whole year's interest charge on the assumption that the cash transaction takes place on the last day of the year.

In the case of discrete receipts and payments of cash, for example on the purchase of an asset or receipt of a grant, this approach would be valid. On the other hand, receipts from sales and the payment of everyday expenses occur continuously throughout the year and the calculation of interest on the last day of the year is less valid.

A PV factor table does exist which is calculated on the assumption that cash flows take place continuously throughout the year rather than on the last day. Ideally we should use both this table and the year-end factor tables in tandem, applying each to the relevant type of cash flow within one project.

In practice firms normally use only one table for all transactions based on the year end convention, as the difference between them is not regarded as significant. Significant differences are more likely to occur where a high discount rate is used over a short life or a low discount rate is used over a long life.

The continuous PV factor table can be used where cash flows are known with a high degree of certainty and exact interest calculations are crucial, as with lease or buy appraisals. The first case study at the end of the book illustrates this particular point.

Project life

It is not always obvious how many years' cash flows should be contained in the appraisal. In the case of cost saving investments, say in the automation of a manual process, the appraisal should be for the life of the new equipment. If this life is longer than will be required then a residual value can be assumed at the end of the project's life and be shown then as a cash inflow.

When appraising new products the project life can be taken as either the product life or the plant life, whichever is the shorter. If the plant life exceeds the product life a residual value can be assumed as above. If the product life exceeds the plant life, the plant replacement can be built into the cash flow in the year required.

In complex production systems all the plant items will not conveniently wear out simultaneously, so a number of replacements may occur in different years. It is important to recognise that for the moment we are still assuming these replacements are at the same prices as the original plant.

Relevant cash flows

Relevant cash flows are all the additional costs and income which will result if the proposed investment goes ahead. These are sometimes called the 'incremental' cash flows as they exclude existing costs on the grounds that they do not result from the investment now being made.

For this reason we do not apportion existing fixed overheads like rent and rates to projects because such costs continue irrespective of this project's acceptance or rejection. They result from previous decisions and should not be charged against a new project.

6. Opportunity costs and sunk costs. An exception to this rule may occur when an existing asset will be sold if the proposed investment does not proceed.

EXAMPLE 4.2

A firm rents premises for £150,000 p.a. but could now sublet an unused part of the buildings for £50,000 or, alternatively, use the space to produce a new product. In this case the £50,000 p.a. is a valid cash flow to include in the new product appraisal. This type of cost is known as the 'opportunity cost' for the obvious reason that it is the cost of the opportunity forgone.

Another example of this opportunity cost frequently occurs when a new project can utilise existing machinery which would otherwise be sold. Here again the sale price of the machinery is taken as a relevant cash flow on this project because a similar amount of cash would have to be spent on another machine if this one had not been available.

It is important to realise that it is the present worth of an existing asset which could be counted as the cash flow. The original cost or written-down value of the asset is irrelevant in an appraisal. Any costs that were incurred in the past are 'sunk costs' and should not affect decisions that are made now. Only the current disposal value, or opportunity cost if put to alternative use, is relevant at this point of time.

EXAMPLE 4.3

A company is considering the production of a new product which will have a five-year life and is expected to show an annual profit of £50,000 based on the following forecast:

	£	£
Selling price per unit		26
Less: Direct labour (3 hours at £3)	9	
Materials (2 kgs at £3)	6	
Overheads	10	25
Profit per unit		£1

Annual forecast sales 50,000 at £1 profit per unit = £50,000

The figure for overheads per unit includes:	£
Variable overheads	2
Depreciation (a)	3
Head office costs (b)	2
Supervision (c)	1
Marketing (d)	2
	£10

Notes:

(*a*) Depreciation represents the cost of the machinery costing £800,000 with an eventual scrap value of £50,000 written off over five years on a straight line basis.

(*b*) Head office costs are based on the normal rate of allocation of $33\frac{1}{3}$ per cent of material costs. The only impact of the new product upon head office costs will be the appointment of a manager and two sales clerks at a total cost of £35,000 per annum.

(*c*) The supervision costs represents the transfer of four

supervisors from another product. Three of these will be replaced by new staff at a salary of £8,000 p.a. each and the fourth, who earns £15,000 p.a. would have been made redundant, with redundancy pay of £20,000.

(*d*) The marketing cost represents the contribution of the new product towards group advertising expenses. In order to promote the new product, additional group advertising of £75,000 has been agreed for each of the next five years.

The cost of capital to the company is 10 per cent and taxation is to be ignored. Calculate whether the new product is worthwhile on the basis of these figures.

(ICSA Business Finance, Dec. 1981)

Solution

This situation calls for the relevant yearly cash flows to be identified over the five-year life and then discounted at the 10 per cent cost of capital to see whether a positive NPV remains, in which case the new product is worthwhile.

Calculation of NPV at 10%

Year	*Annual cash flow* £000	*PV Factor at 10%*	*Present value* £000
0	– 780	1.000	– 780
1–5	+301	3.790	+1,141
5	+ 50	.621	+ 31
		NPV	+ £392

We can conclude from the relatively large net present value surplus of £392,000 that this new investment is worthwhile. The cash flows used in the above appraisal do illustrate many of the points previously made about the relevance of costs and the following notes explain the principles involved:

(*i*) Year 0 cash flow is the net figure of the £800,000 cost of new machinery less the £20,000 redundancy pay saved.

(*ii*) Years 1–5 comprise:

			£
Sales			1,300,000
Less:	Direct labour	450,000	
	Materials	300,000	
	Variable overheads	100,000	
	Head office costs	35,000	
	Supervision	39,000	
	Marketing	75,000	
			999,000
Yearly cash inflow			£301,000

Depreciation is ignored as a yearly cost as the cost is shown at Year 0 on purchase and we should not double count the same cost.

Head office costs are shown at their incremental cost of £35,000 as any reallocation of existing costs via a general overhead recovery rate is irrelevant.

Supervision is charged at the opportunity cost or actual salaries of the four staff involved. Not having to make the redundancy payment of £20,000 is a saving in Year 0.

Marketing costs incurred for this product are the incremental advertising costs of £75,000 only. Existing group advertising costs are irrelevant to the decision as they will continue even if this product is rejected.

(*iii*) The scrap value of £50,000 is shown as a cash inflow in Year 5 when it will be received.

Project teams

On relatively small projects only one manager may be involved in assessing the future benefits of a proposed investment. Take the proposal to install a conveyor system to replace manual handling. An industrial engineer can probably assess the expected yearly savings over the equipment's life.

In contrast, a project to build and equip a factory to sell new products is not within the compass of any one individual. A project team of an engineer, a production manager, a sales manager and an accountant may be needed to assess the yearly cash flows.

Data on past performance may be useful but the application of scientific management will be more beneficial in assessing future costs and benefits. The techniques of market research, method study, work measurement and value engineering are only some of those relevant to new investments and will be employed by project teams.

Summary

In this chapter we have identified the principles governing the cash flows used in investment appraisals. We have seen that only incremental costs are relevant to a new project and that sunk costs are irrelevant to the appraisal. The only exception to this rule is where a sunk cost has an opportunity cost in an alternative use.

We have also seen that profit and cash flow are conceptually different, both in timing and content. In particular the depreciation charged in a profit and loss account is ignored when compiling expenses for the annual cash flow.

Until now it has been useful to assume that only one estimate of future cash flows is made. When we examine the problem of uncertainty later, we will relax this assumption and examine the idea of producing a number of sets of cash flows based on different assumptions. Similarly we will also look at the impact of taxation and inflation on cash flows in later chapters.

Progress test 4

1. Explain why cash flows, rather than profits, are used in DCF calculations.

2. A firm buys a piece of office equipment with a life expectancy of 10 years but expects to resell it at the end of 6 years. What life will the project appraisal be conducted over?

3. A firm bought a vehicle 3 years ago for £9,000 for use on a project now completed. Its book value is now £2,700. A motor dealer has valued it at £2,300 and offered to buy it at that price. An alternative use could be found for the vehicle on a new project currently being appraised. What value should be placed on the vehicle for this purpose?

4. Explain why existing fixed overhead costs are excluded from any new project appraisal.

5 Specific examples of appraisals

Having examined the nature of relevant cash flows for projects in general, we now want to construct the yearly cash flows for specific investment situations. Most capital investments have a common pattern in that the initial investment at Year 0, and sometimes for a further year or two, is followed by cash inflows for most of the subsequent years.

Different investment criteria will be assumed to demonstrate the use of the various appraisal techniques in practice. Sometimes a conflict between multiple criteria may arise where a particular project satisfies one criterion but fails to satisfy another.

For example, a project may be expected to reach the desired rate of return but fail on the speed with which payback is completed. We therefore need to examine the claims to superiority of the different criteria which we do first in the classical investment situation of a new product appraisal.

New product appraisal

This situation calls for an initial investment in fixed assets such as plant, machinery, equipment and, possibly, new buildings or extensions to existing ones. Should replacements of plant and vehicles be required during the period covered by the appraisal then these are fed in as a cash outflow in that particular year. Scrap or disposal values of fixed assets are shown as a cash inflow in the last year of the project's life, or in the subsequent year if that reflects the time it will take to dismantle or dispose of a particular asset.

Any initial working capital requirements are shown as a cash outflow at Year 0 and any additional amounts required in later years are similarly shown as an outflow in the year it occurs. All working capital recoverable is shown as a cash inflow in the last year of the project's life on the grounds that stocks will be depleted towards the end of the last year and debtors will pay within a very short time after the last year end.

Cash inflows from the trading activity are the net amount from sales less all variable costs of labour, materials and variable overheads together with any incremental or specific fixed overheads incurred solely for the project being appraised.

EXAMPLE 5.1

The management of Expansion Ltd are considering investing £80,000 in new plant and £20,000 in working capital to make and sell a new product. Profits before charging depreciation are expected to be £45,000 in each of the four years the product will be sold.

At the end of two years some plant replacement will be required at a cost of £20,000. After four years it is estimated that the plant can be sold for £10,000 and the working capital released in full.

Expansion Ltd require a return of at least 20 per cent on a discounted cash flow basis before approving projects of this kind. They also look for an undiscounted payback period of two years maximum.

Calculation of the NPV at 20%

Year	*Investment*	*Profit*	*Net cash flow*	*PV factors at 20%*	*PV*
	£	£	£		£
0	–100,000		–100,000	1.000	–100,000
1		+45,000	+ 45,000	.833	+ 37,485
2	– 20,000	+45,000	+ 25,000	.694	+ 17,350
3		+45,000	+ 45,000	.579	+ 26,055
4	+ 30,000	+45,000	+ 75,000	.482	+ 36,150
				NPV	+£17,040

Solution

The initial investment at Year 0 is £100,000, being the £80,000 spent on the plant and £20,000 on working capital items such as stocks and debtors. This working capital of £20,000 needs to earn a return just as much as the investment in fixed assets as it is employed in the business until the end of Year 4. Together with the £10,000 sale proceeds of the plant, the £20,000 working capital is shown as a total cash inflow of £30,000 at the end of Year 4.

Cash inflows from sales less costs amount to £45,000 each year. Depreciation is not charged as the whole cost of the plant is charged as a cash outflow when it occurs at Year 0.

The NPV surplus of £17,040 indicates the company can expect a greater return than the 20 per cent required. By a further trial rate and interpolation of the two NPVs the DCF yield can be found at 28 per cent. Expansion Ltd will consider this project to be viable on this criterion as the expected return of 28 per cent exceeds their minimum target figure of 20 per cent. However, the project fails to satisfy the payback criterion of two years, taking nearly three years of the undiscounted cash flows to recover the initial £100,000 invested and the subsequent £20,000 spent on plant renewal.

The decision whether to proceed with this investment or not now rests on which criterion is regarded as the primary one or whether both are equally regarded. In the latter case the new product introduction will be rejected as it fails one of the two tests.

The question of primacy among criteria is for each firm to decide for itself. Assuming the required return of 20 per cent allows for Expansion Ltd's cost of capital then any return in excess of this adds to its wealth and such projects are worthwhile.

The problem for firms is that sometimes a worthwhile project when viewed over its whole life may not be attractive when viewed over a shorter term. This is a shortsighted view but an understandable one as companies and their management tend to be judged by investors on their immediate performance.

Another point to consider is the reason for the setting of a payback criterion. It does not measure profitability in any way but merely the speed with which cash flow returns the original investment.

Firms often use payback with two points in mind. One relates to risk, on the premise that uncertainty increases with time. The other relates to a shortage of capital for investment purposes and the use of payback to ration out scarce funds.

Such use may not lead to the most profitable allocation of funds, which we discuss in more detail later. It does, however, ensure a more rapid turnover of capital, as funds repaid within a year or two from the one project are quickly reinvested in the next project. As mentioned in the previous chapter, a survey of investment practices of large companies found that about one third of the sample regarded payback as a top priority.

Cost saving investment

This investment is usually associated with the purchase of equipment with a view to making savings in operating costs. In this age of the second industrial revolution, obvious examples are the introduction of robotics in a factory, the change to point-of-sale stock control in a hypermarket, and the use of information technology in an office.

The justification for the initial capital investment is a saving in the annual operating costs of the particular task performed. Such savings are calculated on an incremental basis by comparing pre-investment operating costs with post-investment operating costs.

For example, if labour costs were £10,000 per annum before the introduction of a new machine and £6,000 afterwards, then the annual saving amounts to £4,000.

EXAMPLE 5.2

Efficient Builders Ltd are contemplating the substitution of hod carriers on their building sites by a mechanical hoist. Their studies have indicated that a machine costing £20,000 will save labour costs of £15,000 each year. Operating and maintenance costs of the machine will amount to £6,000 in each of the five years the machine is expected to last. At the end of this time the machine is not expected to have any remaining value and will be scrapped. The directors do not normally approve expenditure unless at least a 25 per cent return on investment is anticipated.

Solution
Calculation of the NPV at 25%

Year	Investment £	Operating cost £	Savings £	Net cash flow £	PV factors at 25%	PV £
0	–20,000			–20,000	1.000	– 20,000
1		–6,000	+15,000	+ 9,000	.800	+ 7,200
2		–6,000	+15,000	+ 9,000	.640	+ 5,760
3		–6,000	+15,000	+ 9,000	.512	+ 4,608
4		–6,000	+15,000	+ 9,000	.410	+ 3,690
5		–6,000	+15,000	+ 9,000	.328	+ 2,952
					NPV	+£4,210

As there is a surplus NPV we can conclude that the net savings of £9,000 in each of five years yields a return in excess of the 25 per cent required. This investment is therefore worthwhile. How profitable the investment is expected to be can be found by calculating the DCF yield. This is easily performed in this case with the cumulative PV table, as there is a constant yearly cash flow.

$$\text{Cumulative PV factor} = \frac{\text{Cost of investment}}{\text{Annual cash flow}}$$

$$= \frac{\pounds 20{,}000}{\pounds 9{,}000} = 2.222$$

When we look for 2.222 on the five-year line of the cumulative PV table in Appendix 3 we find it equates to a DCF yield of 35 per cent.

Rather than pin all our faith on one precise estimate of savings, it is sometimes easier to turn the question round and calculate the value of savings required to achieve the 25 per cent return required. To do this we again use the cumulative PV table and turn the formula around.

$$\text{Annual savings required} = \frac{\text{Cost of investment}}{\text{Cumulative PV factor at 25\%}}$$

$$= \frac{\pounds 20{,}000}{2.689} = \pounds 7{,}438 \text{ p.a.}$$

As the operating costs are £6,000 each year this means that savings in hod carriers' wages must exceed £13,438 each year before the investment will be worthwhile. Managers may find it easier to answer a question posed in this way rather than be asked to plump for one exact estimate of savings.

Replacement investment

You may think that a replacement decision is another cost saving investment, and in many ways it is similar to the previous example. In that case the decision was whether to invest or not. Assuming that the underlying activity is still required, a replacement decision is a choice both whether and when to invest. Replacement is normally indicated when the first year saving gives an adequate return if repeated over the whole life of the new asset.

EXAMPLE 5.3
Modern Ltd are considering replacing an existing machine with a new one to reduce operating and maintenance costs. The new machine will cost £40,000 and is expected to last ten years before being scrapped. The existing machine can be sold now for £5,000. Operating and maintenance costs are currently £25,000 for the existing machine, but will fall to only £18,000 each year for the new machine. Modern Ltd require a return of at least 15 per cent before sanctioning such investments.

Solution
Calculation of NPV at 15%

Year	*Existing costs*	*New costs*	*Net cash flow*	*PV factors at 15%*	*PV*
	£	£	£		£
0	– 5,000	– 40,000	– 35,000	1.000	– 35,000
1–10	– 25,000	– 18,000	+ 7,000	5.019	+ 35,133
				NPV	+ £133

This modernisation scheme results in annual savings of £7,000 on the incremental investment of £35,000 comprising the cost of the new machine less the resale value of the old one. This gives a NPV surplus of only £133, which means that the DCF yield will be almost exactly the 15 per cent rate used. The proposal to replace the machine is therefore very marginal as it is expected to yield only the minimum required return.

1. Other aspects. Replacement situations are not always so easy to evaluate. We may be faced with increasing running costs as each machine gets older. These future costs must therefore be estimated. It may be necessary to repair or overhaul the existing machine to extend its useful life. These repair and overhaul costs need to be assessed.

Any such extended life of the existing machine is unlikely to be as long as the life of a new machine. Ways have to be found to compare like with like over a common period. This can be effected either by comparing their total PV costs over the lowest common denominator number of years, or by comparing their costs-in-use on an annual basis. These techniques are illustrated in the later chapter on life-cycle costing.

A further complication can arise if an improved specification will be available if replacement is deferred for another year or two. When appraising replacement situations the alternative courses of action must be identified and costs and benefits assessed. Care must be taken to ensure the comparisons are valid and the above points considered where relevant.

Case Study No. 2 examines a replacement situation where running costs increase each year and the life of the replacement machine exceeds that of the existing machine.

Mutually exclusive investments

In Chapter 3 we saw that projects can be ranked in order of attractiveness, either by the size of the DCF yield or by the profitability index on the NPV method. Care must be taken when selecting the best investment from a range of alternatives because these two indicators do not necessarily lead to the correct choice in this limited situation.

Alternative investments occur when the acceptance of one project precludes the acceptance of an alternative scheme to achieve similar ends. Such investments are referred to as being 'mutually exclusive'.

The basic rule to follow is to choose the alternative with the highest

NPV surplus in absolute terms, when discounted at the required rate of return. An equally valid approach is to calculate the return on the extra or incremental capital cost of the dearer alternative to decide if it is worth spending the extra money. Example 5.4 demonstrates these methods.

EXAMPLE 5.4

Carriers Ltd are trying to decide between two transporters which are both satisfactory from a technical viewpoint but which have different costs and benefits. Model A costs £40,000 and its payload is expected to earn £10,200 in each of the next ten years. Model B costs £30,000 but its earning capacity is only £8,400 each year for the same life. Carriers Ltd management do not know their cost of capital but want to know which transporter is the better buy.

Solution

Summary of DCF yields and NPVs at varying rates

	Year 0 £	Years 1–10 £	DCF yield	NPV at 30% £	NPV at 20% £	NPV at 8% £
Model A	−40,000	+10,200	22%	−8,462	+2,758	+28,442
Model B	−30,000	+ 8,400	25%	−4,027	+5,213	+26,364
Increment	−10,000	+ 1,800	12%	−4,435	− 2,455	+ 2,078

The above analysis shows that Model A gives a DCF yield of 22 per cent whilst Model B gives a return of 25 per cent. If Carriers Ltd require a return on new investments higher than 25 per cent, then neither of these two investments is satisfactory. This is also illustrated by both NPVs being negative at the 30 per cent higher rate assumed.

However, at a lower required rate of say 20 per cent both projects appear satisfactory as they have positive NPVs and their DCF yields exceed this target figure. Model B has the higher NPV surplus at this rate and will therefore be the one selected when we apply the rule for mutually exclusive investments.

Should the required rate for Carriers Ltd be relatively low, at say 8 per cent, then the higher NPV surplus is now achieved by Model A notwithstanding that its DCF yield at 22 per cent is less than the 25 per cent of Model B.

This apparent paradox can be explained by looking at the

difference in costs and revenues of the two models. The incremental investment cost of Model A over B is £10,000 for which the incremental return is £1,800 each year. Over a ten-year life this gives a DCF yield of 12 per cent.

We can think of Model A as being the combination of Model B and the increment. Both their DCF yields of 25 per cent and 12 per cent respectively exceed the 8 per cent postulated. Therefore Model A is preferred because it achieves everything that Model B offers and in addition it earns an acceptable return on the extra £10,000.

If the required return were set higher than the 12 per cent achieved by the incremental investment then this would not be the case and Model B would now be preferred. This would then leave the firm with £10,000 to invest in another project which satisfied the higher criterion rate of 12 per cent plus.

Example 5.5 typifies a practical situation where a choice between alternatives must be made.

EXAMPLE 5.5

The board of Pilmar Plastics Ltd is considering whether or not to replace equipment used in the manufacture of a particular type of television case. It is estimated that the remaining life of this product is five years and that at the end of that time any equipment held will be valueless. The selling price of the case is £5.00 and sales of 20,000 units per annum are expected over the next five years.

Three alternatives have been suggested by the chief production engineer:

A Persisting with the existing equipment which originally cost £60,000 five years ago and which is being depreciated at 10 per cent per year on a straight line basis. The total annual cost of this method including depreciation is £95,000. This method has a continuing investment in working capital of £20,000.

B Purchase of new equipment which would cost £300,000. In this case there would be a trade-in allowance of £50,000 on the old equipment. This method requires a total investment in working capital of £40,000 and the total annual cost, including depreciation, would be £82,000.

C Sale of the existing equipment to Biret (Gloucester) Ltd for £20,000 plus a royalty of 25p on each case sold over the next five years. Biret expects to sell 20,000 units per annum. The cost of capital used by Pilmar Plastics Ltd for appraising capital proposals is 15 per cent.

Required:

(*a*) Show by computation which of the three alternatives A, B or C offers the most attractive proposition for Pilmar Plastics Ltd (ignore taxation).

(*b*) Comment on the implications of the information produced in your answer to (*a*).

(Certified Diploma)

Solution

The basis of choice between these three alternatives is to select the one offering the highest NPV surplus after the yearly cash flows have been discounted at the 15 per cent cost of capital for Pilmar.

Both the original cost of the equipment and the £20,000 existing working capital are ignored as they are 'sunk costs' common to all three situations. Any new investment in equipment or working capital must be taken into account, as must be the sale or release of any investment at the appropriate time. Depreciation must be excluded from costs as it is not a cash transaction. The calculations are:

Option A: NPV = + £46,812 i.e. (£11,000 x 3.352) + (£20,000 x 0.497)
Option B: NPV = + £11,336 i.e. £270,000 investment at Year 0 less (£78,000 x 3.352) + (£40,000 x 0.497)
Option C: NPV = + £56,760 i.e. £40,000 + (£5,000 x 3.352)

These NPV calculations suggest that the highest return will be found from ceasing manufacture now and selling out to Biret Ltd, taking royalties on future sales. This Option C yields £10,000 more present value than continuing to manufacture with the old equipment (A) and £45,000 more than would result from buying new equipment (B).

A further advantage of Option C is that the risk element is minimised. The royalty payment is based on unit sales irrespective of changes in costs or selling prices and will only vary with demand, as it would on all alternatives.

Lease or buy decision

It is important to separate this decision from the underlying one of the asset acquisition. The initial decision is based on whether the benefits justify the purchase cost of the asset, or not. If this test is passed, the supplementary decision is whether to purchase outright or to pay by instalments over the years.

We separate these two decisions to overcome a problem first mentioned in the introductory chapter. This stated that we would not want to reject a project one month because it happened to be financed by an expensive source of funds only to accept a similar project the following month which was to be financed from a cheaper source.

To avoid this illogical situation we regard all finance as contributing to a common pool out of which all projects are financed at the same average cost of capital.

When we examine the alternative methods of financing the acquisition of an asset we are again choosing between mutually exclusive investments. The basic rule we normally follow in this kind of situation is to choose the investment with the highest NPV surplus. However, as we will ignore all the benefits from the use of the asset on the grounds that they are common to both methods of financing, we are examining costs only in the lease or buy appraisal. The more attractive option therefore is the one with the least NPV cost. This is the decision rule we follow.

EXAMPLE 5.6

Modern Ltd has decided to acquire the replacement machine mentioned in a previous example at a net cost of £35,000. The manufacturer has offered leasing terms as an alternative to outright leasing terms as an alternative to outright purchase. The leasing agreement stipulates ten yearly payments of £6,500 payable at the start of each year. Modern Ltd's cost of capital is 15 per cent.

Solution

Calculation of the NPV of leasing payments at 15%

Year	Cash flow	PV factor at 15%		PV
	£			£
0	-6,500	1.000		- 6,500
1-9	-6,500	4.772		- 31,018
			NPV	- £37,518

The present value cost of the ten leasing payments is £37,518 after allowing for 15 per cent interest. This is some £2,500 more than the cost of outright purchase and leasing is therefore not an attractive option. A proviso here might occur if the firm was short of capital and could earn a better return on the £35,000 which will be tied up on the outright purchase option.

Another way of thinking about the NPV of the leasing payments is that £37,518 is the sum of money needed to withdraw £6,500 immediately for the first payment and £6,500 at the end of each of the next nine years. This is made possible by the balance earning interest at 15 per cent per annum until the next instalment is withdrawn each year.

2. Timing of lease payments. The exact timing of leasing payments within each year is very critical to lease or buy decisions. If say the leasing payments had been made at the end of each year then the total NPV cost would amount to only £32,623 which is now cheaper than outright purchase.

It is more likely in practice that the leasing payments will be made periodically throughout the year. In this case their NPV cost amounts to £33,676 which is found by use of a further table not illustrated in this book. These further tables allowing interest calculations for weekly, monthly or quarterly leasing payments are required in practice for accurate results.

3. Taxation. Non-taxpaying organisations will appraise the choice between lease or buy in the above manner. In the past they have found leasing terms attractive when they reflect the tax allowances obtainable by the finance company which are denied to themselves. Case Study No. 1 includes tax aspects in a lease or buy appraisal as it applies to private sector firms. It also discusses further the timing of leasing payments.

Capital rationing

When firms have access to unlimited funds then any investment which is expected to achieve the required rate of return can proceed. Only projects whose NPV is negative, or whose DCF yield is less than the minimum required return, will be rejected. In this context it does not matter whether we evaluate projects by their NPV or DCF yield as the only test of viability is whether they match the minimum required return.

Funds are not always in plentiful supply, however, and may be insufficient to allow all profitable projects to proceed. This occurs when the owners have already invested all their capital in the business and do not wish to borrow nor dilute their ownership.

Small companies are often in this situation. Here the firms will grow at the pace dictated by the size of retained profits as this is the only source of additional capital. Larger companies may also face a shortage of funds if they are already highly geared, or when market conditions do not allow the raising of new share capital at that time.

Faced with the constraint of a capital shortage a firm has to ration out the available funds on the most profitable projects. Now we face the same problem as we did in the case of mutually exclusive projects, namely that the projects with the highest DCF yields are not necessarily the ones to choose. For example, a 30 per cent return for three years is not as good as a 29 per cent return for a longer period.

4. Rationing rule. The best way to ration out scarce capital is to use the profitability index method previously mentioned in Chapter 3. This relates the NPV of the cash inflows to the NPV of the initial outflow(s). The higher the index number then the more cash is earned for every pound invested, after deducting interest for the waiting time at the firm's cost of capital.

EXAMPLE 5.7
Farlon Ltd has only £190,000 to invest with no access to further funds. It is faced with five possible investments A, B, C, D and E, all of which are viable at the 15 per cent required rate of return

but which have a total initial outlay of £390,000. Details of these five projects and their NPVs, DCF yields and profitability indices are:

	Project				
	A	B	C	D	E
Project life	2yrs	5yrs	5yrs	4yrs	5yrs
Year	£	£	£	£	£
0	−100,000	−120,000	− 50,000	− 90,000	− 30,000
1	+ 69,440	+ 38,400	+17,100	+ 36,100	+ 10,900
2	+ 69,440	+ 38,400	+17,100	+ 36,100	+ 10,900
3	—	+ 38,400	+17,100	+ 36,100	+ 10,900
4	—	+ 38,400	+17,100	+ 36,100	+ 10,900
5	—	+ 38,400	+17,100	—	+ 10,900
NPV at 15%	+12,909	+ 8,717	+ 7,319	+ 13,066	+ 6,537
DCF yield	25%	18%	21%	22%	24%
Profitability index	1.129	1.073	1.146	1.145	1.218

According to which of the above three criteria is used, the ranking of the five projects will be in the order:

Ranking method	Ranking order
NPV at 15%	D,A,B,C,E
DCF yield	A,E,D,C,B
Profitability index	E,C,D,A,B

Solution

Projects must have an index number greater than 1.000 to be viable. Funds are allocated to projects starting with the highest profitability index number first, then descending in rank order until the capital is exhausted or until the cut-off point of an index number of 1.000 is reached.

This firm has insufficient capital to undertake all five investments and therefore the ranking method is important as different rankings produce different total NPVs.

Let us assume that none of the projects is mutually exclusive and that any project is divisible into fractions for ease of explanation. Farlon Ltd will maximize the total NPV surplus on its limited funds when it allocates the scarce capital to projects by the size of their profitability index rather than the size of their NPV or DCF yield. This is verified in Figure 5.1.

	Ranking by NPV surplus			Ranking by DCF yield			Ranking by profitability index	
	Outlay	NPV		Outlay	NPV		Outlay	NPV
D	90,000	13,066	A	100,000	12,909	E	30,000	6,537
A	100,000	12,909	E	30,000	6,537	C	50,000	7,319
B	—	—	2/3 D	60,000	8,711	D	90,000	13,066
C	—	—	C	—	—	1/5A	20,000	2,582
E	—	—	B	—	—	B	—	—
	190,000	25,975		190,000	28,157		190,000	29,504

Figure 5.1 *Comparison of NPVs using different ranking methods*

The profitability index gives the combination of projects which yields the largest NPV surplus at the 15 per cent required rate of return. The other two criteria can never select a group of projects to yield a higher NPV than that found by the profitability index.

It is possible for a firm to face more than one constraint simultaneously. For example, it may face both a shortage of funds and a shortage of a particular resource which cannot be overcome in the short term. It will then be necessary to use operational research techniques to find the most worthwhile mix of projects. This use of management science will also be necessary should a firm face a multi-period capital rationing situation as the technique described above applies to single period rationing only.

Further conflict

Sometimes a further constraint on the selection of profitable projects occurs when there is a requirement that profits should never fall below a certain absolute level in the profit and loss account, or alternatively, below a certain percentage return on capital. This may lead to a conflict of objectives in the short term due to investments not being immediately profitable, although perfectly viable over their whole life.

EXAMPLE 5.8

Last year a firm made profits of £2m on capital employed of £10m giving a return on capital of 20 per cent. This situation is expected to continue in future years. A new project is proposed which will require the investment of £1m now and a further £1.5m in one year's time. Profits in the second and subsequent years are expected to be £1m per annum on the new project with a DCF yield of about 30 per cent. The pre and post-investment performance can be summarised as follows:

Year	*Capital employed*	*Profit*	*Return on capital*
	£	£	%
–1	10m	2m	20
0	11m	2m	18
1	12.5m	2m	16
2	12.5m	3m	24

The effect of the new project initially is to increase the capital employed as the new project is developed, but to add nothing to profits in the first year, hence the fall in the return on capital from 20 per cent to 16 per cent. Once the new project earns profit on its own account in Year 2, it raises the overall return on capital to 24 per cent. This is a significantly higher level than before because the DCF yield is substantially higher than the pre-existing return on capital.

Situations where this kind of conflict occurs are when top management are judged on profit and loss account performance, either by a parent company or by stock market investors in the case of a plc. A case can be made and the owners prepared for the short-term effects, but if the owners are disinterested in longer-term gain and judge purely on short-term results then some profitable opportunities may have to be forgone.

Summary

This chapter identified a number of types of investment and illustrated appraisals for new product, cost saving, replacement and lease or buy situations. We have also seen that special rules are necessary in one or two cases where conflict can arise between criteria in the choice of the best projects.

These situations specifically relate to mutually exclusive investments where the decision rule is to choose the alternative with the highest NPV surplus in absolute money terms. The other situation requiring a special rule is where funds are not available to finance all possible projects and the capital has to be rationed out. Here we use the size of the profitability index to rank projects in order of their attractiveness until the funds are used up.

In the next chapter we introduce the corporation tax system as it applies to profit-seeking organisations in the UK and specifically show how it is incorporated in discounted cash flow appraisals.

Progress test 5

1. Mechtek Co. are considering investing £30,000 in new equipment to make a component used in one of their products. Additional working capital of £5,000 to finance stocks and work-in-progress will also be required during the eight-year life of the equipment. At present the 3,000 components used each year are bought in at £7 each. The variable costs of production are estimated at £4 per component. Mechtek Co. have a cost of capital of 15%. Advise the company whether or not this investment is worthwhile.

2. RentProp Developers are planning to build an office block on a site they will acquire for £0.5m. If they build Design A at a cost of £4m the available space can be let for £1m p.a. Alternatively, a larger Design B can be built for £5m when the available space could be let for £1.3m p.a. In both cases the building life is put at 40 years. The company's cost of capital is 18%. Which design should they choose?

3. Would you lease or buy the £35,000 machine in Example 5.6 if the annual lease payments were £7,000 for the first five years and £2,500 for the last five years, all payable at the start of each year? The cost of capital is 12%.

4. Any one of the following three investments would use up the total amount of capital available to spend this year. The cost of capital is 14%. Which investment would you choose and why?

Investment	*Capital cost*	*Annual cash flow*	*Life*
A	£90,000	£25,000	10 yrs
B	£80,000	£26,000	8 yrs
C	£87,000	£20,000	11 yrs

5. The DCF yield on a £6m investment has been calculated at 20% plus. It will take three years to construct involving equal capital expenditures in each year, all financed by 12% long term loans.

Explain how the project may not look attractive over the next three years from the viewpoint of overall company return on capital, even though it is worthwhile on a long term view.

6

Incorporating taxation

Tax rates and tax allowances have both come down from the high levels of the 70s and early 80s in the UK, although this was partly at the expense of a tax allowance called 'stock relief' which was discontinued in 1984. Even now, a corporation tax rate of 35 per cent is not insignificant and forms an important part of the economic environment in which investment decisions are made.

The value and timing of tax transactions do affect the rate of return on any investment, albeit not so significantly as when 100 per cent tax allowances on plant and machinery were available.

The existence of a central government with the power to levy taxes means that it can try to influence firms' investment decisions through the tax system. Managers should be aware of the significance of these tax matters and how they affect their firms. If we ignore taxation in both its timing and value, we do not fully appraise investment opportunities.

Cash flows on any project will be incomplete if we do not build the tax effects into the yearly figures. There are two aspects of taxation, one being negative and the other positive. The negative side is the payment of tax on profits whilst the positive side is the receipt of tax allowances which in effect reduce the size of the tax payments.

Corporation tax

Corporation tax is the system of taxation which applies to profits of all limited companies and nationalised industries, as opposed to income tax which applies to profits of partnerships and the self-employed.

Differences between the two systems are confined mainly to the tax rates and the timing of the tax payments. We shall concentrate on the principles of corporation tax first then a comparison with the income tax system can be made later.

There are two rates of corporation tax, either of which can apply, depending on the size of the taxable profit for the year. The normal rate is 35 per cent at the time of writing but a small companies rate of 25 per cent exists for firms whose profits are relatively low.

There is a gradual increase in the rate from 25 per cent to 35 per cent which applies to companies whose profits fall within the band where the 25 per cent rate ceases to apply but the full 35 per cent rate is not yet applicable. Often the Chancellor changes these limits and sometimes the actual rates of tax. Even when the rates are altered it is normally too late for a company to take avoiding action as the March budget announcement of the rates of tax is within a week or two of the end of the fiscal year to which it relates.

1. Accounting and tax years. The accounting year for many companies will not cover the same twelve months as the tax year which runs from 1 April one year to 31 March of the following year. If the rate of tax did alter from one tax year to the next and the company accounting year straddled both tax years, then the year's profit is apportioned pro rata for the number of months which fall into each tax year. The two rates of tax can then be levied on the respective part of the profit which falls into each tax year.

EXAMPLE 6.1

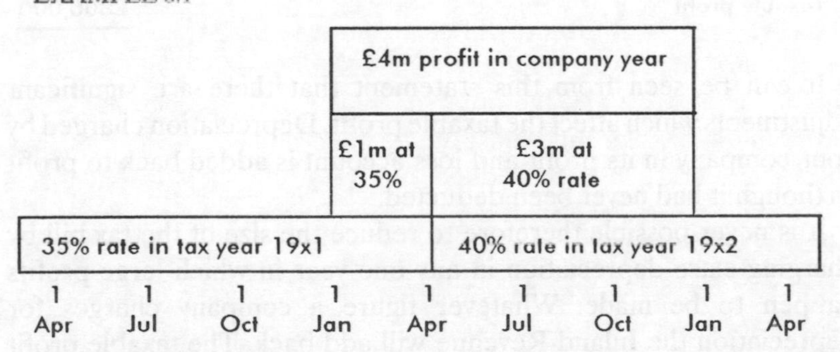

A company's accounting year runs from 1 January to 31 December during which time it made a taxable profit of £4m. This accounting year straddled two tax years between which the rate of corporation tax changed from 35 per cent to 40 per cent. The profit will be apportioned pro rata so that three months will be charged at 35 per cent and the other nine months at 40 per cent as shown.

Taxable profit

The profit on which corporation tax is levied (£4m in the above example) is not identical with the profit disclosed in the firm's profit and loss account but is an adjusted profit figure after some costs have been disallowed and some allowances received. The following corporation tax assessment shows the main adjustments that take place:

Corporation tax assessment

		£
Profit as per profit and loss account		900,000
Add back disallowed expenses:	£	
Depreciation	200,000	
Entertainment	10,000	
Political contributions	5,000	
Provision for possible bad debts	1,000	216,000
		1,116,000
Deduct: Capital allowances		316,000
Taxable profit		£800,000

It can be seen from this statement that there are significant adjustments which affect the taxable profit. Depreciation charged by your company in its profit and loss account is added back to profit as though it had never been deducted.

It is never possible therefore to reduce the size of the tax bill by charging extra depreciation in any one year in which large profits happen to be made. Whatever figure a company charges for depreciation the Inland Revenue will add back. The taxable profit each year is sales less all allowable operating costs excluding depreciation.

EXAMPLE 6.2

Referring back to the first example in Chapter 4, a firm invested £100,000 in new plant which it decided to depreciate at £25,000 p.a. over the next four years. Sales revenue amounts to £200,000 p.a. whilst labour and material costs amount to £150,000 p.a. The yearly profit amounts to £25,000 but the taxable profit is the same as the yearly cash flow, in this instance £50,000.

If a firm leased the physical assets then the leasing or hiring payments are included as expenses in the profit and loss account and tax relief is granted automatically. When a firm purchases these same assets itself, the pro rata charge called depreciation is included in each year's profit and loss account which the Inland Revenue ignore, substituting their own capital allowance in its place.

Depreciation methods

To understand how tax allowances are calculated we first need to understand the two main ways in which depreciation is calculated in the UK. Both methods take the original cost of the asset, its estimated life, and any scrap or residual value at the end of that life into account.

EXAMPLE 6.3

A machine costs £11,000 and has an estimated resale value of £1,000 at the end of its five-year life with the company.

	Reducing Balance method £	*Straight line method* £
Original cost	11,000	11,000
First year depreciation (38%:18.18%)	4,180	2,000
Balance sheet value-end Year 1	6,820	9,000
Second year depreciation (38%:18.18%)	2,592	2,000
Balance sheet value-end Year 2	4,228	7,000
Third year depreciation (38%:18.18%)	1,607	2,000
Balance sheet value-end Year 3	2,621	5,000
Fourth year depreciation (38%:18.18%)	996	2,000
Balance sheet value-end Year 4	1,625	3,000
Fifth year depreciation (38%:18.18%)	618	2,000
Balance sheet value-end Year 5	1,007	1,000

One method charges an equal annual amount of depreciation in each year and is known as the 'straight line method'. The other charges a lesser amount of depreciation as each year goes by, and is known as the 'reducing balance method'. See Example 6.3.

The choice of depreciation method to be used in a company's profit and loss account lies between straight line and reducing balance. This choice is partly at the discretion of the particular company's management insofar as the guidelines spelled out in Statement of Standard Accounting Practice No. 12 allow.

Capital allowances

Whichever method is chosen it is unlikely to coincide with the Inland Revenue's calculation of the capital allowance. An exception perhaps is the case of motor vehicles where many firms use a 25 per cent reducing balance rate for depreciation purposes which is identical with the rate of capital allowance.

EXAMPLE 6.4
25% capital allowances/depreciation on an £8,000 car

	£	
Purchase cost of car	8,000	
Year 1 — capital allowance	2,000	(25% of £8,000)
Written down value — Year 1	6,000	
Year 2 — capital allowance	1,500	(25% of £6,000)
Written down value — Year 2	4,500	
Year 3 — capital allowance	1,125	(25% of £4,500)
Written down value — Year 3	3,375	

Whenever an asset is sold a balancing up with the Inland Revenue takes place. If we assume the above car was sold after three years' use it is unlikely it would exactly realise its book value of £3,375. If it was sold for £3,000 the Inland Revenue would give an additional capital allowance of the £375 difference, which is termed a 'balancing allowance'.

Conversely, if the car realised £3,800 on disposal the taxman would claim back the excess allowance of £425 previously granted which is termed a 'balancing charge'.

The following is a list of the current rates of capital allowances:

Rates of capital allowances as at February 1989

Industrial buildings	4% annual allowance on a straight line basis for 25 years.
Plant and machinery	25% annual allowance on a reducing balance basis.
Motor vehicles	25% annual allowance on a reducing balance basis.

When appraising projects, the availability of these tax allowances must be incorporated in the cash flows for any tax-paying organisation. The tax saved by offsetting these allowances against profits occurs in the year the payment would otherwise have taken place. We now must look to see when tax is due for payment.

Tax payments

One of the good things we can say about tax on limited company profits is that it is not payable immediately, but after a time lag. The present system of corporation tax goes back to 1972 and is called an 'imputation system'.

When a limited company makes a dividend payment it pays a 'net' dividend to shareholders and a tax payment to the Inland Revenue. For example, on a gross dividend of £1,000 the tax payment is £250 at a standard rate of 25 per cent. Such tax is deemed to be an advance payment of the company's total corporation tax liability for the year.

The shareholder receives a net dividend of £750 but his income is imputed to be this amount plus the tax credit of £250 which the company paid on his behalf. The same tax of £250 therefore performs two functions. It satisfies the income tax levied on a shareholder's dividends and it forms part of the corporation tax levied on the company's profit. If this was otherwise it would mean the same profits would be taxed twice, once in the company's hands and again as income in shareholders' hands should that profit be distributed.

Most companies make not just one but two dividend payments

relating to any one year's profits. The first dividend payment may be made towards the end of the accounting year after the directors have deliberated on the first six months' results. The second dividend payment is likely to occur after the annual general meeting has agreed the directors' dividend recommendation and this will be some months into the next accounting year.

This results in two payments of 'advance corporation tax' at the time of the interim and final dividend payments. These two ACT payments are deducted from the total tax liability for the year and the balance or 'mainstream' tax liability can be assessed. However, this payment will not actually be made until nine months after the accounting year end when the March 1987 Budget is finally implemented.

The nature of these three tax payments, all relating to the profit of any one year, makes it very difficult to generalise about exactly when tax is paid. It depends on the timing and size of dividend payments, and on when the company was formed.

2. Incorporating tax payments. When appraising investments we need to incorporate tax payments in the yearly cash flows. A good rule of thumb is to assume that a delay of one year occurs for all tax payments.

EXAMPLE 6.5

Assume a company makes taxable profits of £500,000 per annum in each of four years. The rate of corporation tax is 35 per cent. The following yearly cash flows emerge when the tax payments are lagged one year:

Year	*Taxable profit*	*Tax at 35%*	*Net cash flow*
	£	£	£
1	+500,000	—	+ 500,000
2	+500,000	–175,000	+ 325,000
3	+500,000	–175,000	+ 325,000
4	+500,000	–175,000	+ 325,000
5	—	–175,000	– 175,000

The appraisal must continue one year further than the life of the investment to take account of the time lag in tax payments.

Because tax payments are made in arrears, the benefit of deducting capital allowances from profits to reduce these tax payments must also be delayed. Any capital allowances a firm can deduct from its year's profit will reduce the mainstream tax payment rather than the ACT payments which are solely dictated by the size of the dividends.

In an individual project appraisal where we need to include as a cash inflow the tax saved by claiming capital allowances, it is necessary to allow either a one- or two-year time lag. This is because the investment takes place at Year 0, being the beginning of the project's first year.

If this time happened to be near the end of the company accounting year the delay could be only nine months. If the investment took place at the start of the company accounting year the tax saving could be twenty-one months away. Within your own company you may be able to make a more precise estimate of these delays in tax transactions, which used to be longer before implementation of the 1987 budget.

3. Taxable entity. Another point to consider is whether firms are taxed project by project or as a total entity. We need to incorporate tax savings and payments in each project appraisal, but in reality firms are taxed on the total profit less allowances for the whole firm. In some cases, a number of firms in one group may be taxed as one entity so that capital allowances of one company can be offset against profits of another should that be necessary.

If the total profit of a firm is large enough to offset all available capital allowances then we do not have to offset the allowances of one project against only that project's profits. We can effect a saving in the tax paid by the whole entity but we show this as a cash inflow on the particular project being appraised.

EXAMPLE 6.6

ABC Ltd invest £1m in new equipment to make and sell a new product, which is expected to earn £500,000 more than its direct costs over each year of its expected four-year life. A capital allowance of 25 per cent on a reducing balance basis is available and the rate of corporation tax is 35 per cent. A balancing allowance will be claimed at the end of Year 4 when the equipment is scrapped. Compile the net cash flows for discounting purposes.

Solution

Computation of net cash flows

Year	Investment	Profit earned	35% tax on profit	Capital allowance	Tax saved on allowance	Net cash flow
	£	£	£		£	£
0	−1,000,000					−1,000,000
1		+500,000		250,000		+ 500,000
2		+500,000	−175,000	187,500	+ 87,500	+ 412,500
3		+500,000	−175,000	140,625	+ 65,625	+ 390,625
4		+500,000	−175,000	421,875	+ 49,219	+ 374,219
5			−175,000		+147,656	− 27,344
						+£650,000

Note that a two-year lag has been assumed for the tax saved by the allowance in the absence of more specific information.

If the benefit gained by saving tax on the allowance had occurred in Year 1 this would only be possible where profits already exist in the rest of the company equal to the size of the allowance claimed. Where there are no other company profits against which to offset the capital allowances of this one project, then the allowances have to be deferred until the project's own profits cover the allowances claimed. This would then appear as illustrated above.

In either case, the total tax payable amounts to the same figure over the project's life, but the ability to claim the tax allowance more quickly will result in a higher DCF yield after discounting.

A comprehensive example of an expansion project incorporating aspects of taxation in an inflationary environment is contained in Case Study No. 3 at the end of this book.

Government assistance

Apart from capital allowances there are one or two other possible sources of financial assistance for new investment, particularly in areas of high unemployment, or for the purpose of introducing new technology.

Should any grant be available on new investment in plant and industrial buildings, for example in an enterprise zone, then this is built into the project's cash flow in the year it is received. Such grants are normally tax free and therefore do not affect the tax payments so should be shown separately from the cash inflows earned from the trading activity.

Another form of financial incentive for new investment is called 'selective assistance' but this is in effect a kind of subsidy and is taxable, so if should therefore be incorporated in the cash inflows which are taxable.

Other incentives apply in particular localities, often to aid small firms and others to create job opportunities. Managers should check out all available sources of assistance before embarking on a new project as prior approval is needed in most instances. Once the value and the timing of the assistance has been determined it is incorporated in the cash flows of the project concerned.

Public authorities

Corporation tax applies to nationalised industries whether privatised or not, and they should allow for the payment of tax and the benefit of capital allowances in their project appraisals in exactly the same way as any other private sector firm.

A situation can arise with some firms, in both public and private sector, where large accumulated capital allowances or trading losses make the payment of corporation tax a very distant possibility. In this case it would be advisable to ignore both tax payments and capital allowances and exclude them from the cash flows used in the calculation of the profitability of the investment. This will also be the way to treat local authorities and similar bodies which are specifically excluded from corporation tax.

Taxing the self-employed

Previous discussion has centred on limited companies which come under the auspices of the corporation tax system. Some businessmen, however, trade in their own name, or as a partnership, without ever forming a limited company.

Profits of these self-employed persons come under the income tax system which also applies to employees. Unlike limited companies, the self-employed do not pay dividends and any drawings or salary they pay themselves are disallowed when computing the taxable profit.

Profits from running a business are deemed to be the income of the individual or partner. Like limited companies, the same capital allowances on new investment apply. The remaining taxable profit is taxed in bands varying from 25 per cent to 40 per cent after the personal allowances for the particular individual have been deducted.

4. Timing of tax payments. Collection of income tax from employees takes place weekly or monthly under the PAYE system. The Inland Revenue cannot operate the same system with self-employed persons because the income or profits are not known until after the accounting year ends. In practice it takes a few months to prepare, audit and agree taxable profits with the taxman.

To overcome this problem the Inland Revenue charges income tax in the current tax year based on the level of profits earned in the previous tax year. More precisely, the normal basis of assessment, for ongoing self-employed firms, is to take the profits of the accounting year ended in the previous tax year as the basis for assessing tax payable in the current tax year. This is known as the 'preceding year' basis.

Because current profits can never be available in time, tax is based on out-of-date figures. This does not mean that there is a long delay in the payment of tax but simply that current tax is based on an out-of-date level of profit. The actual payment of tax is made 50 per cent on 1 January in the current tax year and the remaining 50 per cent on 1 July which actually falls in the next tax year.

EXAMPLE 6.7

A self-employed person ends his accounting year on 31 August each year. The taxable profit after allowances for his year ended 31 August 1987 amounts to £20,000 and falls within the tax year 1987/88. This profit will be used as the basis for assessing income tax for the tax year 1988/89 which tax will be payable half on 1 January 1989 and the remainder on 1 July 1989.

When incorporating tax payments and savings into discounted cash flow appraisals the timing must be taken into account. If profits are constant each year then the correct amount of tax will be paid within three months of the year end and no delay in payment should be assumed. Tax in this case is a cash outflow in the same year as the profit (before charging depreciation) is shown as a cash inflow.

This is not the same case as limited companies where we assume a delay of one year in the payment of tax. In the case of self-employed persons there is no delay of one year but the size of the previous year's profits determines the size of the current year's tax payment. A time lag of one year should be assumed, however, when incorporating the benefit of capital allowances into the net cash flows.

A practical difficulty occurs here when the size of the profits is such that higher rates of tax are payable. The benefit of capital allowances shows up in reduced taxable profits, starting at the highest rate of tax which would have been payable if the investment had not taken place. If the amount of capital allowances is such that a number of bands of taxable income are eliminated, then the tax saved should be calculated at the different marginal rates of tax applicable in that case.

Capital gains tax (CGT)

A capital gain takes place when a possession like a building is sold either for more than the firm paid for it or its market value at 31 March 1982 if that results in a smaller gain or loss. Such a gain is taxable at the going rate of income or corporation tax after an allowance for inflation has been deducted. In the case of a limited company any CGT is included in the corporation tax assessment but a self-employed person will receive a separate CGT assessment. CGT does not apply to profits made from the firm's normal trading activity but only includes profits from the sale of fixed assets and investments.

In practice firms rarely pay this tax because of 'roll-over relief' which allows them to buy new fixed assets of any kind with the total sale proceeds of the old. This defers the tax on the original capital gain until the new acquisition is eventually disposed of in its turn. As this process can be repeated without limit, CGT is not normally a problem for companies or self-employed individuals.

An exception might occur on the 'sale and leaseback' of freehold premises if the firm needs the sale proceeds to pay off debts or increase its working capital as opposed to buying new fixed assets. In this case CGT will be payable, as roll-over relief does not apply.

Value added tax (VAT)

This tax has little influence on investment decisions. Cash flows on a project should be expressed net of any VAT as the tax paid on purchased items is offset against tax charged on sales to customers. The company merely acts as a tax collector when it pays over the balance of tax to the Customs and Excise each quarter.

It is possible for a firm to be out of pocket temporarily if it pays VAT on suppliers' invoices before it receives VAT from its own customers. In this case, additional working capital may be required and should be incorporated in the cash flows of the relevant projects.

Summary

When appraising the worthwhileness of any investment, the effects of tax must be taken into account by profit seeking organisations. Tax allowances and payments pull in opposite directions but their existence and timing can significantly affect the rate of return on a project.

Managers should be aware of these consequences of government intervention and take them fully into account in their decision-making role. This same comment applies to inflation, to which topic we turn next.

Progress test 6

1. 'Tax is just another type of cash flow and should be treated as such in project appraisals'. Explain.
2. Explain the relationship between tax years, accounting years and project years in the context of a project appraisal.
3. 'If the Inland Revenue disallow depreciation, firms are being taxed on profits they have not earned'. Discuss.
4. What is the capital allowance in Year 3 on an investment in new equipment costing £25,000?
5. Reappraise Example 6.6 assuming now the new equipment costs £1.4m and the rate of corporation tax is 30%. All other data remains the same as before.
6. How can public authorities get the benefit of tax allowances when they are excluded from the tax system?

7. Compare and contrast income tax with corporation tax relating to the inclusion of tax transactions in project appraisals.

Success in Investment by R. G. Winfield and S. J. Curry 4E 1991 23 Units p 426
Beginners' guide to investment by Bernard Gray 2E 1993 21C p 433 £13

7

Allowing for inflation

Unfortunately inflation is like the poor – always with us. Economic historians can point to times past when the value of money actually increased but these have been short-lived. In the present inflationary era we need to be able to distinguish between the apparent return on an investment and its real return after allowing for inflation.

First we examine some of the broader issues of inflation accounting before homing in on how to deal with it on specific project appraisals.

Problems of inflation

Inflation has been present in the UK , as in the world economy, throughout the whole post-war period. When the rate of inflation was at a mild rate of less than 5 per cent per annum, accountants and others largely ignored its existence when preparing financial statements.

Over a number of years, however, even a modest rate of inflation like 5 per cent per annum has a dramatic effect on the value of the assets of a firm. Even more important is the effect on the replacement cost of such assets when they eventually wear out and have to be renewed.

The basic problems presented by inflation when preparing financial statements are that profits are overstated in the profit and loss account, and asset values are understated in the balance sheet. This leads to an incorrect assessment of the return on capital earned by the business and makes real performance hard to measure.

In terms of the day-to-day running of the business there is also the danger that current selling prices may not reflect the up-to-date costs of stock and asset replacements.

If this is the case, cash earned by the business may often be insufficient at times of high inflation to pay taxes, reward investors and finance these higher replacement costs of stock and plant. Very often it is the latter which have suffered and the firm reinvests too little, either to finance inflation or to allow real growth.

In the 1970s, the rate of inflation in the UK rose into double figures, and by the mid-70s, and again at the start of the 80s, threatened to turn us into a banana republic. This concentrated the minds of the accountancy bodies and various government-appointed committees to agree eventually on the following system of inflation accounting.

Inflation accounting

More properly inflation accounting is called 'current cost accounting' and a specific procedure for accountants to follow was set out in Statement of Standard Accounting Practice No. 16 entitled 'Current Cost Accounting'.

This statement required public listed companies to clarify the effects of inflation on both the profit earned in the year and on the values of assets held at the year end. These procedures were to be followed for a three-year experimental period in the early 1980s.

This period has now ended and the statement has now lapsed until such time as the accountancy profession agree on the best course of action. It is perhaps fair to say that the technicality of the subject matter did not endear it to the investing public at large or to top management. Interest therefore waned when inflation fell back to relatively low levels by the mid-80s.

However, it is useful to review past procedures aimed at quantifying the effects of inflation to get a feel for its far-reaching effects.

1. Current cost accounting. Profit and loss accounts and balance sheets are normally prepared on the basis of the original cost of the items, which is referred to as the 'historic cost' convention. A 'current cost' profit and loss account takes the historic cost profit and makes several adjustments to allow for the various effects of inflation before arriving at the real profit attributable to the owners.

It would be very optimistic to assume that company managers, investors, employees and possibly even accountants understand all the ramifications of these adjustments. The effects of inflation on pricing policy, working capital requirements, corporation tax assessments, dividend policy, the cost of capital and wage claims are complex and not easily understood.

EXAMPLE 7.1

Current cost profit and loss account

		£000
Profit as in 'historic cost' profit and loss account		1,000
Deduct:	(*a*) Depreciation adjustment being the extra cost of depreciation calculated on the replacement cost instead of original cost.	(200)
	(*b*) Cost of sales adjustment being the extra cash needed to replace stocks at prices ruling at the time of sale.	(300)
	(*c*) Monetary working capital adjustment being the extra cash needed to give credit to customers for the value of goods which have cost more to produce.	(100)
		400
Add back:	The proportion of the above adjustments (*a*), (*b*) and (*c*) not required to be borne by the owners if part of the firm's capital is borrowed (assumed 50% of 600 here).	300
	= Real profit earned for owners	700

The tendency is for companies, unions and the financial press to concentrate on the well-known misleading figures and ignore attempts to produce more realistic ones. In 1986 there were many examples of companies, previously in the vanguard of inflation accounting reporting, now reverting to historic cost accounts alone in their published accounts.

2. Effect on cost of capital. Managers should be aware that inflation also increases the cost of capital. Interest rates on borrowed capital are partly influenced by the rate of inflation but more so by government action to contain it. Shareholders expect partial if not complete protection of their dividend income from the erosive effects of inflation.

As the required or target rate of return must reflect these inflationary expectations then the conclusion must be that we should not invest in projects that do not meet this inflated minimum rate of return. To do otherwise will not lead to the real growth of the firm but the opposite.

Having looked at the general problems caused by inflation it is now time to look more specifically at the effects of inflation on a single project's profitability.

Effects of inflation on project appraisals

Until now, the investment appraisal techniques discussed in previous chapters have implicitly ignored the existence of inflation and its effects on the future cash flows of projects being appraised. It would be a happier world for managers if this absence of inflation could be justified. Unfortunately, inflation exists in the real world, and although the rate of inflation may fluctuate from year to year, few pundits are forecasting its complete demise.

Inflation brings additional problems to project appraisals. It increases the uncertainty and makes more difficult the estimation of the future cash flows including sales revenue, operating costs and working capital requirements. As we shall see it also influences the required rate of return through its effects on the cost of capital.

In the context of investment appraisals it means that two aspects of the value of money must be considered. The time value of money has already been catered for by the use of present value factors which deduct interest for the time elapsed when waiting for future cash receipts. The other aspect is the change in the value of money itself, not because of the time lapse, but because the inflationary process decreases its purchasing power.

Real and nominal rates of return

When describing how to allow for inflation in investment appraisals, and cope with both these aspects, it is useful first to distinguish between the 'real' rate of return on a project and its 'nominal' rate of return. A simple example may clarify this difference between real and nominal rates of return:

EXAMPLE 7.2
Suppose an investor receives an income of £100 p.a. on an investment of £1,000, then the nominal rate of return is 10 per cent. If inflation is zero, then the real rate of return will also be 10 per cent. However, if inflation is running at 6 per cent p.a., then the real rate of return is approximately the nominal rate of 10 per cent minus the 6 per cent rate of inflation, which leaves only 4 per cent.

Again, if inflation is running at 15 per cent p.a., then the nominal rate of return of 10 per cent is swamped by inflation resulting in a negative real rate of return of about 5 per cent. To summarise:

Approximate relationship of real and nominal returns

Nominal return %	*Rate of inflation* %	*Real return* %
10	nil	10
10	6	4
10	15	(5)

Note: the more accurate relationship is found from the formula:

$$\text{Real rate of return} = \frac{\text{Nominal rate of return}}{\text{Rate of inflation}}$$

$$\text{For example } 1.038 \text{ (i.e. 4\%)} = \frac{1.10}{1.06}$$

This experience of negative real returns was all too vivid for small investors in the late 1970s when the rate of inflation frequently exceeded the rate of interest received on bank or building society deposits. This trend has been reversed in the 1980s when the rate of interest receivable has exceeded the rate of inflation by a few percentage points and investors received a positive real return again.

3. Business rates of return. Turning to an industrial context, a company's rate of return on investment is the annual after-tax profit expressed as a percentage of the capital employed in the business. This is a nominal rate of return. The real return on investment will be this nominal return less the rate of inflation.

The real and nominal rates of return referred to here for the whole company are not strictly correct, because the concept of profit is not identical with that of cash flow. This is partly because of the different treatment of depreciation but also because profit ignores the timing of cash receipts and payments and can arise when cash is not even received.

4. Project rates of return. It is important to recognise that the company's one year return on investment is conceptually different from the whole life project return based on the timing of cash flows. It is far from uncommon for a wholly satisfactory project with a high estimated return to have an adverse effect on the company profit and loss account, particularly in the first year or two. One reason is because the initial investment costs show as depreciation and interest charges before revenue starts to flow and profits are earned. An example in Chapter 5 illustrated this effect.

In the case of individual project appraisals, the nominal rate of return is the apparent DCF yield found when discounting future cash flows that have been inflated to take account of anticipated inflation. The real rate of return on such a project, however, is this nominal rate of return minus the rate of inflation. If future cash flows on a project have been expressed in the constant value of Year 0 purchasing power, then the solution DCF yield is the real rate of return. A later chapter further discusses real versus nominal rates of return and also explains how part of the effects of inflation are borne by the providers of loan capital and are not therefore totally borne by the owners of a company.

Quantifying the effects of inflation

At appraisal time managers are faced with the choice whether to express future cash flows at their inflated values and find the nominal rate of return, or alternatively to express them in the constant purchasing power as at Year 0 and find the real rate of return.

What influences managers as to which choice to make depends on how top management express the target rate of return and whether managers see the future cash flows keeping pace with inflation or not. If firms express the target rate of return in nominal rather than real terms this is likely to be because the target rate of return is often based on the cost of borrowing or the opportunity cost of alternative financial investments, both of which are expressed in nominal terms.

5. Zero inflation. The effects of inflation can best be illustrated by a series of short, simple examples, all based on the same data but varied for different assumptions for the effects of inflation. We start this process on the assumption of a zero rate of inflation.

EXAMPLE 7.3

An investment of £97,170 has a four-year life and generates sales revenue of £100,000 p.a. with labour, material, etc. costs of £70,000 p.a. to give a profit (before charging depreciation) of £30,000 p.a. Taxation and working capital are initially excluded for ease of illustration.

Rate of return assuming zero inflation

Year	Capital cost	Sales revenue	Labour, material, etc	Net cash flows	PV factors at 9%	PV
	£	£	£	£		£
0	– 97,170			– 97,170	1.000	– 97,170
1		+100,000	–70,000	+30,000	.917	+27,510
2		+100,000	–70,000	+30,000	.842	+25,260
3		+100,000	–70,000	+30,000	.772	+23,160
4		+100,000	–70,000	+30,000	.708	+21,240
					NPV	0

The nominal rate of return on this project is 9 per cent, which is also the real rate of return when inflation is zero.

6. Keeping pace with inflation. If all cash flows on a project are affected equally by inflation, and at the same time, then there is no effect on the real rate of return. On revenue-earning projects this assumes that selling prices rise at the same rate as costs without any time lag. In the case of cost-saving projects this assumes, justifiably in most cases, that the increased costs to be saved will keep pace with the general inflation rate. In both cases it is assumed no significant working capital is involved.

When this assumption of keeping pace with inflation can be made, then the firm can express the future cash flows in the constant purchasing power of Year 0 and discount to find the real rate of return. The nominal rate of return on such a project is this real rate plus the expected rate of inflation. The real rate of return may turn out to appear relatively low.

When the zero inflation assumption is relaxed there are only two possible outcomes. Either the cash flows on the project will keep pace with inflation or they will not. We will take the former case first.

EXAMPLE 7.4

It is now assumed that inflation proceeds at 10 per cent p.a. on a compound basis and that both costs and revenues increase at the same pace.

Rate of return assuming 10% inflation on all cash flows

Year	*Capital cost*	*Sales revenue*	*Labour, material, etc.*	*Net cash flows*	*PV factors at 20%*	*PV*
	£	£	£	£		£
0	- 97,170			- 97,170	1.000	- 97,170
1		+110,000	- 77,000	+33,000	.833	+27,489
2		+121,000	- 84,700	+36,300	.694	+25,192
3		+133,100	- 93,170	+39,930	.579	+23,119
4		+146,410	-102,487	+43,923	.482	+21,171
					NPV	- £199

Given the scale of the figures, the NPV deficit of £199 is negligible, so we can take the nominal rate of return on this same project now to be 20 per cent. This is equivalent to the same real rate of return of 9 per cent as found in the previous example when we convert by the formula on a previous page.

$$\text{Real rate of return } 9\% \text{ (i.e. } 1.09) = \frac{\text{Nominal rate of return } (1.20)}{\text{Rate of inflation } (1.10)}$$

The above assumption of the future cash flows keeping pace with inflation is shown not to affect the real rate of return. If this was always the case then inflation would not be a problem in project appraisals.

An alternative approach is sometimes used and involves a double discounting exercise. The inflated net cash flows in the last example can be discounted by 10 per cent PV factors to bring them back to constant Year 0 purchasing power. This would result in the net cash flows as shown in the first example which are then discounted to find that the real rate of return is still 9 per cent.

7. Differential inflation. The other possible outcome is that the cash flows on the project do not keep pace with inflation. Some of the costs and revenues may be inflating at different rates to others on the same project. Other cash flows, like tax saved on capital allowances, do not inflate at all.

This lack of synchronisation has been the experience in the UK when, for example, wages have tended over the years to outstrip prices in general. In this situation the manager has to inflate each component cash flow separately to build up the future annual net cash flows. These future cash flows can then be discounted to find the nominal rate of return from which the real rate of return can be deduced if required. This is shown in Example 7.5.

EXAMPLE 7.5

To illustrate this situation it is now assumed that the general rate of inflation is 10 per cent p.a. and that costs increase at the same rate whilst sales revenue increases by only 7 per cent p.a.

Rate of return assuming differential inflation

Year	*Capital cost*	*Sales revenue*	*Labour, material, etc.*	*Net cash flows*	*PV factors at 8%*	*PV*
	£	£	£	£		£
0	−97,170			− 97,170	1.000	− 97,170
1		+107,000	− 77,000	+30,000	.926	+27,780
2		+114,490	− 84,700	+29,790	.857	+25,530
3		+122,500	− 93,170	+29,330	.794	+23,288
4		+131,080	− 102,487	+28,593	.735	+21,016
					NPV	+ £444

Again, the NPV is insignificant given the scale of the figures so we can conclude that the nominal rate of return on this project is about 8 per cent, which is equivalent to a real rate of return of about –2 per cent when inflation is 10 per cent.

Clearly the effect of this differential inflation on revenue and costs has had a dramatic effect on profitability. What might have seemed to be just a marginal slippage, of sales revenue against costs, more than halved the nominal rate of return from 20 per cent to 8 per cent. It also completely eliminated the real rate of return which was as high as 9 per cent when sales revenue was assumed to keep pace with inflation as illustrated in the prior example.

On revenue-earning projects the greater the differential effect, either by costs increasing faster than revenue or some costs increasing faster than the general rate of inflation, then the greater the effect on the real rate of return. Just imagine the effect on the real rate of return of sales held constant by a fixed price contract that had not included an allowance for inflation when the contract was negotiated!

EXAMPLE 7.6

Let us continue with the basic example now assuming that costs are inflating at the general rate of 10 per cent p.a. whilst sales revenue is held constant on a fixed price contract.

Rate of return on a fixed price contract

Year	*Capital cost* £	*Sales revenue* £	*Labour materials, etc* £	*Net cash flows* £
0	–97,170			– 97,170
1		+100,000	– 77,000	+ 23,000
2		+100,000	– 84,700	+ 15,300
3		+100,000	– 93,170	+ 6,830
4		+100,000	–102,487	– 2,487
				– £54,527

In this case the cash inflows do not recover the original investment resulting in a total loss of £54,527. This is before any discounting takes place to account for the time value of money. In other words, the nominal rate of return is negative and the real rate of return even more so.

Effects of inflation on working capital

Inflation creates cash flow problems for firms. Not only is the replacement cost of fixed assets increased but, usually more important, extra cash is needed each and every year to finance the increased money value of working capital.

This extra cash is needed to finance the increased labour, material and overhead costs which are normally paid for, long before the money is recovered from customers. Free credit from suppliers also increases in money value with inflation and this helps to offset the increase in a firm's own working capital items of stocks and debtors.

At times of high inflation and recession, the silly situation can be reached whereby a firm can produce and sell less products but still need more working capital. This occurs when the percentage rate of inflation on its costs exceeds the percentage decrease in the volume of activity.

The original example used in this chapter assumed an investment of £97,170 excluding working capital. It would be more realistic to suppose that some additional investment is needed for working capital, i.e. to finance stocks and give credit to customers.

Assuming stock levels are financed by creditors, this leaves debtors to be financed by the firm itself. With a sales level of £100,000 we might anticipate no more than £20,000 being owed by customers at any time. Therefore the working capital required at the start of the project will be £20,000 and will remain at this figure over the whole life of the project provided sales volume and selling prices remain constant.

We also assumed a constant volume of sales in our basic model so that increased sales value was attributed to higher selling prices caused by inflation. What effect has this on the working capital requirements of the firm? The £20,000 working capital that was adequate with zero inflation will now need to be topped up each year as shown in Example 7.7. This is because the credit given to customers represents the increasing costs of labour, materials and overheads already paid for by the firm.

In general, the greater the rate of inflation and the longer the life of the project the more topping up will working capital need.

Apart from this cash-flow problem, the other effect will be on the profitability of the project. Interest will have to be paid or forgone on the extra money tied up in working capital each year. Therefore the rate of return on this project will be reduced, whatever the rate of inflation, compared with the same project when inflation did not exist.

EXAMPLE 7.7
Using the assumption of 10 per cent per annum inflation with all cash flows keeping pace, the £20,000 working capital will need the following increases:

Working capital requirements with 10% inflation

Year	*Sales level for coming year*	*Total working capital required (assumed=20% sales)*	*Change in working capital required increase (decrease)*
	£	£	£
0	110,000	22,000	22,000
1	121,000	24,200	2,200
2	133,100	26,620	2,420
3	146,410	29,282	2,662
4	—	—	(29,282)

Over the life of this short project nearly 50 per cent more cash is needed for working capital than would be the case if inflation did not exist and the original £20,000 sufficed.

Our earlier assumption that the real return on a project is not affected by inflation, provided sales revenue keeps pace with inflation, should now be modified. Although sales revenue may keep pace, the cash flows do not, because extra working capital is required each year.

Effects of inflation on taxation

We considered in an earlier chapter how the two aspects of taxation are built into the net cash flows of a project. On the one hand companies make tax payments based on the previous year's profit. On the other hand, the size of that taxable profit is reduced by capital allowances on new investment. What effects has inflation on these tax transactions? The answer is a mix of beneficial and adverse effects.

Tax payments are based on the adjusted historic cost profit and no additional tax is levied by the Inland Revenue to compensate for the average time lag of about one year. The payment of tax by companies is therefore favourably affected by inflation as the retarded payment reduces its real cost.

Capital allowances on industrial buildings, motor vehicles, plant and equipment reduce the size of the taxable profits and their benefit is reduced in real value by the same time lag as the tax payment.

When assets are being depreciated for tax purposes at a 25 per cent p.a. rate on reducing balance, then the bulk of the allowances are received within a few years of purchase and inflation will not make serious inroads into their real worth. In the case of industrial buildings when a 4 per cent p.a. allowance is received in each of 25 years, the real value of these allowances will be considerably diminished after only the first few years.

Case Study No. 3 deals with an expansion project and demonstrates the combined effects of inflation and taxation.

Estimating future inflation

The previous discussions on inflating future cash flows may have sounded all too easy to do in principle but do we really need to try to estimate inflation over the next few years? There are a few ways we can tackle this question.

In some cases there is no need to estimate the effects of inflation at all if the assumption that cash flows will keep pace with inflation can realistically be made. This applies when selling price can be immediately adjusted to recover increased costs without loss of volume, or, on cost saving schemes, where the costs to be saved would normally keep in step with inflation. This latter situation of cost savings keeping pace with inflation would be a valid assumption in many cases.

This leaves projects with a differential effect or with a significant working capital requirement. Very few managers would want to forecast inflation rates more than one year ahead but nearly all projects are going to last more than one year. It would be valid to estimate inflation at different rates in different years but few managers could attempt such sophistications.

What we can do on important projects is to test how sensitive the return is to different assumptions of inflation rates. This turns the problem the other way around. Instead of having to forecast future inflation rates we can calculate what rate of inflation would make a project no longer viable. We can then use our judgement to decide whether such a rate is, or rates are, likely to occur. In effect, inflation is just another of those uncertainties surrounding future events and should be treated as such.

Large terminal values

When thinking personally about the effects of inflation one tends to think of house or other property values. These assets have tended to keep pace and often to exceed the general rate of inflation. There is a danger that some commercial and industrial projects may be thought to be viable on the strength of a large rise in the residual value of an asset rather than on the profits earned from the basic trading activity.

A case in point may arise in the brewing industry when an investment to refurbish a public house may appear to be justified on the grounds of increased trade and an enhanced terminal property value. The danger here is that the increased trade may not justify the investment in the refurbishing cost but the enhanced property value might.

Breweries facing this situation should ask themselves whether they are operating in the brewing industry or in property development. The refurbishing cost should be justified by the extra profits from the increased trade alone during the expected life of the refurbishment, leaving out property values. This is because when investments are being appraised we are concerned only with the extra (or incremental) cash flows. Those cash flows which do not result from the investment decision should be ignored. Case Study No. 5 illustrates this aspect of an investment concerning a large inflated terminal value.

Summary

In the real world the effects of inflation on a project's viability must be considered. The target rate of return should be looked at each year in the light of inflationary expectations when expressed as a nominal rate of return.

Cash flows on a project that can be expected to keep pace with inflation can be expressed in Year 0 value £s and the resultant real DCF yield modified to a nominal rate if required by adding the general rate of inflation.

When cash flows on a project are not expected to synchronise with inflation generally they can be inflated at the estimated rate(s) and discounted to find the nominal DCF yield. This can then be compared with the nominal target rate of return.

An alternative approach to estimating future inflation rates is to turn the problem round to test how sensitive the DCF yield is to various inflation rates. This will then highlight at what inflation rate a project becomes no longer viable and managers can use their judgement as to whether such events are likely to occur.

We now go on to look at the whole question of risk and reward and the trade-off between them.

Progress test 7

1. Compare and contrast 'current cost accounting' with 'historic cost accounting'.
2. Explain the difference between a nominal rate of return and a real rate of return in general terms.
3. (*a*) What is the nominal rate of return on an investment when the real rate of return is 9% and inflation is 6%?

   (*b*) What is the rate of inflation when the nominal rate of return is 19% and the real rate of return is 10.5%?
4. What factors determine whether to express future cash flows at todays prices or at future prices?
5. Explain the term 'differential inflation'.
6. Why does a firm need more working capital each year for an investment to make and sell the same yearly quantity of products?
7. Explain how the effects of inflation on the tax cash flows of an investment can be both favourable and unfavourable to a limited company.

8

The cost of capital

Capital is not free. Financial institutions and shareholders expect a return on their investment in the company. In its turn, the company must earn a return on projects at least equal to this cost of capital. To do otherwise will not satisfy the providers of that capital and make the raising of future capital more difficult.

Previous chapters have assumed various discount rates for firms when appraising projects. We now need to examine just how firms should set the minimum required rate of return from new investments. This will vary from firm to firm and industry to industry, but once found, it will serve as the discount rate to use in NPV calculations when testing for viability. Updating may be required in later years should capital market conditions and economic environment change significantly.

Sources of capital

Firms have two main sources of new capital for new investments. They can either borrow the money, usually from a financial institution, or they can obtain it from the owners in one of two ways.

Companies occasionally sell new shares to existing shareholders on a 'rights' issue. This may be unpopular as it tends to depress the existing share price, although in reality a shareholder is no worse off provided he takes up his new entitlement. The other way companies obtain new capital from the owners is by not paying out all the profits earned as dividends. By this means, companies are assured of the extra capital they need and they save the expense of issuing new shares.

1. Capital gearing. Most firms use a mix of borrowed and owners' capital and the relationship between the two is known as 'capital gearing'. A company is said to be highly geared when it has a large amount of borrowed capital relative to owners' capital. It is lowly geared when the proportion of borrowed capital is small.

The relationship between these two sources of capital can alternatively be expressed by calculating each source as a proportion of the total capital.

EXAMPLE 8.1
Levels of gearing

	Low gearing	*High gearing*
Shareholders funds (share capital + retained profit)	90%	50%
Borrowed capital	10%	50%
Total capital	100%	100%

There is no one particular level of capital gearing that is regarded as satisfactory for all companies. Each firm is examined on its past record, future prospects and the security of the interest and capital repayments.

In most industries the 50 per cent borrowed capital indicated above would be regarded as high gearing, although higher rates may be exceptionally found in, say, property development. In a survey by Fox in 1977, 86 per cent of the quoted companies sampled had a gearing ratio of less than 50 per cent.

It is possible to find examples of companies with no borrowed capital, resulting from a policy decision by management to fund growth internally from retained profits. Such companies eliminate the risks of defaulting on the loan or interest payments, or having to reduce dividends when profits fall to meet the prior claim of interest charges.

On the other hand, ungeared companies miss the opportunity of increasing the return to shareholders by investing borrowed capital to earn more than the cost of the interest as shown in Example 8.2.

EXAMPLE 8.2
We take two companies, one with nil gearing and the other with a moderately high level of 37 per cent. Profits of £600,000 are first

shown as a return on shareholders' funds and then recalculated on double the original profit.

	Nil gearing £000	*High gearing* £000
Capital structure:		
Shareholders' funds	4,000	2,500
10% loan	—	1,500
	4,000	4,000
Profit of £600,000		
Profit	600	600
Interest	—	150
	600	450
Corporation tax at 35%	210	157
Earnings	390	293
Return on shareholders' funds	9.75%	11.7%
Profit of £1,200,000		
Profit	1,200	1,200
Interest	—	150
	1,200	1,050
Corporation tax at 35%	420	367
Earnings	780	683
Return on shareholders' funds	19.5%	27.3%

When a company has no gearing the change in profit results in the same proportionate change in the return on shareholders' funds from 9.75 to 19.5 per cent. However, the doubling of profit in the high gearing example more than doubles the return on ordinary shareholders' funds from 11.7 to 27.3 per cent.

Most firms decide that a judicious amount of borrowed capital is beneficial and try to adhere to a target range of gearing over the years. It may be that in any one year the target is exceeded slightly because conditions in the capital markets prevent a particular kind of funding. This can be redressed when market conditions allow.

2. Weighted average cost of capital. Provided the company does not allow its gearing level to become too high, so introducing financial risk to the ever present commercial risk, the overall cost of capital can be kept at an optimal level. New projects must be financed by new capital as the existing capital is usually already invested. We therefore need to look at the cost and the mix of new capital to calculate their weighted average cost which becomes the minimum required return on any new investment.

In doing this we must bear in mind the effects of taxation and inflation on each type of capital as they differ in certain respects. We will first examine the cost of borrowed capital, then the cost of equity, and finally weight the different proportions to get the overall cost. To form a picture of where we end up it may be useful to look at a simple example of the weighted average cost of capital.

EXAMPLE 8.3

A firm has a 30 per gearing level and pays 7.8 per cent net of tax for its borrowed funds. Its shareholders expect a return of 22 per cent on their funds.

Calculation of the weighted average cost of capital

Type of capital	*Proportion*		*Cost*		*Weighted cost*
Loan capital	0.3	x	7.8%	=	2.3%
Shareholders' funds	0.7	x	22.0%	=	15.4%
	1.0				17.7%

The cost of borrowed capital

The rate of interest which has to be paid on new loans to get them taken up by investors at par can be regarded as the cost of borrowed capital. Such rates of interest vary over time in sympathy with interest rates obtainable on alternative investments in the capital markets. They also vary slightly according to the size of the loan and the degree of risk attached to the particular firm.

3. Cost of irredeemable loans. When a firm already has existing quoted loans or debentures, an alternative approach can be used to find the cost of borrowing. If the fixed rate of interest on such loans is less than the current going rate, these securities will have a market price of less than the par value of the stock. Assuming first that the loan is irredeemable or very many years away from now, then the interest yield at the current market price should equate to the current market rate of interest on similar securities.

EXAMPLE 8.4

An irredeemable 9 per cent loan stock is currently quoted at £75 per £100 nominal value of the stock.

$$\text{Market rate of interest} = \frac{\text{Nominal value}}{\text{Market value}} \times \text{Old interest rate}$$

$$= \frac{£100}{£75} \times 9\% = 12\%$$

4. Cost of redeemable loans. When a loan stock is redeemable within a few years, investors will obtain an annual return from the interest payments and also a capital gain on the eventual repayment of the stock at par. The return on the investment can be regarded as the DCF yield as it is for industrial investments.

EXAMPLE 8.5

X Ltd has a 10% loan stock standing at £83 per £100 nominal value, repayable at par in five years time. An investor today is therefore willing to pay £83 for the right to receive £10 yearly interest and £100 back at the end of five years.

Calculation of the DCF yield

Year	*Cash flow* £	*PV factors at 15%*	*PV* £
0	– 83	1.000	– 83.00
1	+10	.870	+ 8.70
2	+10	.756	+ 7.56
3	+10	.658	+ 6.58
4	+10	.572	+ 5.72
5	+110	.497	+54.67
		NPV	+£0.23

The NPV is so negligible we can say the DCF yield, and therefore the current rate of interest, is exactly 15 per cent. This is not to say that every investor will receive a return of 15 per cent as income tax and capital gains tax bear differently on each person.

The DCF yield of 15 per cent obtained by the investor buying an existing loan stock can be regarded as the current cost of interest on new loans issued at par. It represents the money or nominal cost of new loans, which is used to calculate the target rate of return in nominal terms.

5. Real cost of loan capital. The real cost of loan capital will be less as investors are not recompensed by the company for the fall in the value of their capital. This was the reason for the 'gearing adjustment' in the current cost profit and loss account illustrated in the previous chapter.

EXAMPLE 8.6

Using the formula from the previous chapter we can convert the 15 per cent nominal cost of loan capital above to a real cost assuming a rate of inflation of 5 per cent as follows:

$$\text{Real cost of loan capital (1.095)} = \frac{\text{Nominal cost (1.15)}}{\text{Rate of inflation (1.05)}}$$

The real cost of loan capital is therefore 9.5% i.e. (1.095 – 1.000) x 100%

In recent years this real cost of loan capital has been positive but in the later 1970s it was actually negative after allowing for the then high rate of inflation and the tax relief next mentioned.

6. Tax relief on interest. Interest on loans, debentures and overdrafts is deductible from profits before calculating the corporation tax charge, whereas dividends are not. In effect tax relief is granted on interest payments which, with corporation tax at 35 per cent, reduces the rate of interest by one third. Example 8.7 illustrates this point.

It can be seen that the two companies with identical total capital and yearly profit do not pay the same tax charge. Company B which financed half its capital requirements with a 10 per cent loan saves £175,000 of the £500,000 interest cost through tax relief. The 10 per cent rate of interest on the loan effectively becomes only 6.5 per cent with tax at 35 per cent on profits. It is not very surprising that firms find gearing attractive when they compare the after-tax cost of loans with the cost of equity capital.

EXAMPLE 8.7
Tax relief on interest payments

	Company A (no gearing)	Company B (50% gearing)
Shareholders' funds	£10m	£5m
10% loan	—	£5m
Total capital	£10m	£10m
Profit before tax and interest	2,000	2,000
Interest on loan	—	500
Profit after interest	2,000	1,500
Corporation tax at 35%	700	525
Tax saved		175
Net of tax interest cost		325
Net of tax rate of interest		6.5%

The cost of equity capital

The equity of a company is its risk capital, embracing ordinary share capital and retained profits which can both be regarded as having the same cost although issue costs of new share capital does increase its cost slightly in practice.

Put simply, the cost of equity is the return shareholders expect the company to earn on their money. It is their estimation, often not scientifically calculated, of the rate of return which will be obtained both from future dividends and an increased share value. The latter can be assumed to arise through profit earned on the retained profit ploughed back as extra capital and reinvested in the business.

Unfortunately, simple concepts are not always so easy to apply in practice and the cost of capital is a favourite battlefield for academics with no one agreed practical solution.

It is possible to calculate the cost of equity as the DCF yield achieved from the estimated stream of future dividends and the increased share value at a future point in time, in much the same way as we calculated the current rate of interest earlier. This would be a logical approach to the valuation of shares in a takeover situation but a company is more likely to use one of the next two approaches for cost of capital purposes.

7. Earnings yield. A popular method in the past was to assume the cost of equity was the 'earnings yield'. This term is akin to the 'dividend yield' but in this case it refers to profit irrespective of whether it is paid out as dividend or retained by the company.

$$\text{Earnings yield} = \frac{\text{Earnings per ordinary share}}{\text{Market price per share}} \%$$

EXAMPLE 8.8

Graham Ltd made a profit of £20m last year which is expected to be maintained. There are 50m ordinary shares in issue and they currently sell at £2 each on the Stock Exchange.

$$\text{Earnings per share (EPS)} = \frac{\text{Profit for year}}{\text{No. of ordinary shares}} = \frac{£20\text{m}}{50\text{m}} = 40\text{p}$$

$$\text{Earnings yield} = \frac{\text{EPS}}{\text{market price}} \% = \frac{40\text{p}}{£2} \% = 20\%$$

The cost of equity for Graham Ltd is 20 per cent by this method.

8. Dividend growth model. A somewhat similar method to calculate the cost of equity capital is based on what is known as Gordon's dividend growth model. This method takes the expected dividend for the coming year and expresses it as a percentage of the current market price to get the dividend yield. To this is added the average growth rate in dividends which is expected in coming years. In terms of a formula:

$$Ke = \frac{Di}{Po} \% + g\,\%$$

Where Ke = % Cost of equity
Di = Next year's dividend
Po = Market price of share
g = % Growth rate of dividends

EXAMPLE 8.9
Graham Ltd currently pay a net dividend of 20p on each ordinary share which is quoted at £2 on the Stock Exchange. Growth of profits and dividends in recent years has averaged 10 per cent and this trend is expected to continue.

The cost of equity using the Gordon formula is therefore:

$$Ke = \frac{Di}{Po}\ \% + g\% = \frac{20p}{£2}\ \% + 10\% = 20\%$$

Although the cost of equity is shown as being equal on both the Gordon dividend growth model and the earnings yield basis, this need not necessarily always be so.

These methods of calculating the cost of equity more accurately refer to the cost of retained earnings as opposed to the cost of new share issues. The only difference is that the cost of the latter should take into account the issue expenses which in effect increase the cost of this source of finance. The above Gordon formula can be adjusted by making Po equal to the issue price net of issue costs. If, say, the issue price of new shares was £1.80 and the issue costs amounted to 5p per share then Po becomes £1.75.

9. Nominal cost of capital. The 20 per cent cost of equity capital above is a nominal rate rather than a real rate of return to investors. It is also an after-tax return as dividends are paid from taxed profits in the UK, unlike interest payments which are allowed against tax. Fortunately UK corporation tax is neutral between profits retained and profits paid out as dividends.

10. Capital asset pricing model. One last way to measure the cost of equity capital is based on an approach called the Capital Asset Pricing Model or CAPM for short. This topic is explored more in the following chapter as it relates to risk but one aspect is relevant here.

The CAPM method divides the return an investor receives on a share into two parts. The first part equates to the return currently available on a risk-free investment, say in government stocks. The other part is a risk premium relating to the degree of risk attaching to an investment in that particular share.

The risk premium is based on the calculation of what is called a beta factor which is the correlation coefficient between the returns on a market portfolio of investments and the returns on the individual share with their respective risks. In effect the beta factor measures the relative riskiness of the returns expected by investors in the share.

To express the cost of equity in terms of a formula we can say:

$$Ke = Rf + B(Rm - Rf)$$

Where	Ke	=	Cost of equity
	Rf	=	Risk free return
	Rm	=	Market portfolio return
	B	=	Beta factor

Where $Rf = 10\%$; $Rm = 18\%$; $B = 0.6$ the cost of equity becomes

Ke	=	Rf	+	B	$(Rm$	–	$Rf)$
14.8%	=	10%	+	0.6	(18%	–	10%)

This CAPM method is conceptually different from the earnings yield and dividend growth approaches in that it specifically attempts to allow for risk, which the other two methods do not, other than what is reflected in the current market price of the share.

It is unlikely that all the above techniques will coincide and yield the same cost of equity. Hopefully, it is also unlikely that there will be very wide differences. We must always remember that a precise calculation will only really matter for marginal projects rather than the vast majority of projects which are either more than marginally profitable, or totally unviable.

Having decided on the cost of equity we can reassure ourselves by conducting a few simple tests. The cost of equity should be more than the pre-tax cost of borrowed capital because of the greater element of risk.

Another comparison we can make is to look at the shareholder's opportunity cost if he made alternative investments. If the cost of equity appears lower than the return achievable on other financial securities of equal or lesser risk, we should go back to the drawing board with our calculations. Either the sums are incorrect or we cannot justify investing more equity capital to achieve a lower return than shareholders expect.

Weighted average cost of capital

We started with the premise that most firms use a mix of borrowed and equity capital to finance new projects. Having determined how their separate costs are calculated we now need to combine them together to obtain the weighted average cost of capital within an acceptable range of gearing levels.

EXAMPLE 8.10

The directors of Milnthorpe Engineering plc are considering the feasibility of issuing 12 per cent debentures at par to raise £1,000,000 for an investment to broaden their product range. The new plant is expected to produce a return of £240,000 per year indefinitely, before tax and interest charges.

The company's existing capital structure is:

	£
Issued ordinary shares (£0.50 nominal value)	3,000,000
Issued 5% preference shares (£1 nominal value)	6,000,000
Reserves	6,000,000
	£15,000,000

The current market values of ordinary and preference shares are £2.00 and £0.80 respectively, and the company's current maintainable earnings before meeting corporation tax at an effective rate of 50 per cent are £3,840,000 per year.

Required:

(*a*) Calculate the weighted average cost of capital before the issue of the debentures.

(*b*) If there is no change in the cost of either equity or preference capital, what would you expect the market value for ordinary shares to be immediately after the issue of the debentures, and what would the weighted average cost of capital be at that time?

(*c*) Discuss the effect of issuing debentures on the weighted average cost of capital of a company.

(Certified Diploma)

Solution

In this context, the cost of equity is taken as the earnings yield. The weighted average cost of capital (WACC) is based on the current market value of the securities rather than their book value to reflect up-to-date costs of capital.

The earnings calculations are:

	Current structure £000	*New structure* £000
Profit pre-tax and interest	3,840	4,080
Less: debenture interest	–	120
Pre-tax profit	3,840	3,960
Less: 50% tax	1,920	1,980
Profit after tax	1,920	1,980
Less: preference dividend	300	300
Earnings for ordinary shareholders	1,620	1,680

The existing WACC is calculated from the total cost of capital expressed as a percentage of the total market value:

	Market value £m	*Cost* £m	*% cost (net)*
Equity	12.0	1.620	13.5
5% preference shares	4.8	300	6.25
	16.8	£1.920	

$$\text{Existing WACC} = \frac{\text{Total cost}}{\text{Total market value}} = \frac{£1.92\text{m}}{£16.8\text{m}}\% = 11.4\%$$

The new total market value for the shares after the debenture issue will be the new figure of earnings capitalised to 100 per cent at the unchanged earnings yield of 13.5 per cent:

$$\text{Total market value} = £1.680\text{m} \times \frac{100}{13.5}\% = £12.444\text{m}$$

$$\text{Market value per share} = \frac{£12.444\text{m}}{6\text{m}} = £2.07 \text{ per share.}$$

The new WACC is calculated from the new total cost of capital expressed as a percentage of the new total market value after the debenture has been issued:

	Market value £m	Cost £m	% cost (net)
Equity	12.444	1.680	13.50
5% preference shares	4.800	.300	6.25
12% debentures	1.000	.060	6.00
	£ 18.244m	£ 2.040m	

$$\text{New WACC} = \frac{£2.040\text{m}}{£18.244\text{m}} \% = 11.2\%$$

The effect of increasing the gearing ratio by borrowing has been to lower the existing WACC from 11.4 per cent to 11.2 per cent. This is brought about by the cost of borrowing (net of tax relief) being substantially lower at 6 per cent than the previous WACC of 11.4 per cent. The fall in WACC may seem small but the amount of new borrowing is only a very small proportion of the existing capital. The more new capital borrowed, then the more it will reduce the new WACC.

Optimal WACC. However this is only true up to a point. There is evidence that the WACC, when plotted on a graph, tends to be saucer-shaped rather than reach an optimal cost at one specific point. However, once shareholders and bankers perceive that the gearing level is too high then the WACC will increase again.

This is caused by the combination of a higher required return on existing equity and higher interest rates on new loans to compensate both parties for higher risk. At this stage further borrowing will not decrease the WACC but actually increase it because of the effect on the existing equity. This can sometimes lead to an extremely high marginal cost of capital on an extra small tranche of borrowing that results in an increase in the cost of all existing equity.

Another view expressed by Modigliani and Miller is that the WACC is constant irrespective of the level of gearing. They argue that any change in the gearing ratio immediately leads to a change in the cost of equity to counter the change in the level of financial risk.

Their proposition assumes some conditions not always present in the real world and there is probably truth in both viewpoints.

Having found its WACC, a company then uses this as the minimum nominal required return on new investments in its discounted cash flow calculations.

Summary

The cost of capital overall is found from the identification of the cost of each different type of capital used. The cost of borrowing is the current market rate of interest for that type of security, which can be derived from existing loans if necessary.

A judicious amount of borrowing introduced into the capital mix can lower the overall or weighted average cost of capital provided the gearing level is not pushed too high. Borrowing is attractive, not just because its interest rate is lower than that of equity, but also because of tax relief on interest payments which does not apply to dividends.

The cost of equity is the return expected by the owners, i.e. shareholders, on their funds invested in the business. There are various ways of indirectly measuring this cost because it is not practicable to ask a wide body of investors the question, even if they could all articulate an answer. We measure the cost of equity either by the earnings yield method, or the dividend growth model or the capital asset pricing model.

All the individual costs of capital are brought together in one overall nominal weighted average cost. This is then used as a cut-off point in the appraisal of new investments as any project which does not yield in excess of its cost of capital is not worthwhile.

11. Specific finance. The only exception to the general rule that all sources of capital contribute to a common pool is where the raising of new finance is conditional on its being used to fund a specific project, and that project only. This may be associated with government assistance for a foreign or regional development. In this case the specific cost of finance is used in the discounting process.

We next examine the problem of risk which is present in nearly all investments and which links in with the cost of capital, as there is a trade-off between risks and rewards.

Reference

R. B. Fox, 'Corporate leverage – a study', MSc Dissertation, University of Bradford, 1977.
Modigliani, F. and Miller, M. H. (1958) 'The cost of capital, corporation finance and the theory of investment', American Economic Review, vol 48.

Progress test 8

1. 'Ungeared firms miss the opportunity of increasing the return on owners' capital. It therefore follows that all firms should have as high a gearing level as possible'. Discuss.
2. Calculate the change in the return on shareholders' funds in Example 8.2 (high gearing case) assuming profit levels of initially £800,000 and then £1,100,000 in place of the £600,000 and the £1,200,000 respectively.
3. Calculate the current rate of interest for a 14% loan stock standing at £130 per £100 nominal value if it is repayable at par (£100) in 10 years time.
4. 'When both inflation and tax relief on interest are taken into account, the real cost of loan capital is cheap'. Discuss.
5. What is the cost of equity for a plc whose shares are quoted at £1.35 when the previous year's dividend was 5p net and in recent years the dividend has increased on average by 12% p.a.?
6. What are the practical limitations on progressively reducing the WACC by increasing the gearing ratio?

9

Risk and uncertainty

It would be unrealistic for us to assume that the future events expressed in yearly cash flows will occur exactly as predicted. The nature of investment appraisal is such that we are dealing with an uncertain future with the risk that one or more of income, costs, tax, inflation or project life may vary from our estimate. Some writers differentiate between risk and uncertainty along the lines that risk can be quantified but uncertainty cannot. It is intended here to use the terms synonymously.

When projects are overwhelmingly profitable it does not matter which appraisal techniques are used as they are viable on any test we care to apply. Most projects, however, are more marginal and subject to a greater degree of uncertainty.

It is here that discounting techniques come into their own by taking into account each year's cash flow over the whole life of the project. This allows us to manipulate the data to answer 'what if' questions and generally apply financial modelling techniques. Computers have an obvious role here when we are dealing with reiterative calculations on raw data. Dedicated programs can be used to calculate NPVs and DCF yields and subsequently test the effects on these of changed assumptions regarding the value of key variables.

Equally useful is to use a general spreadsheet for these applications. Spreadsheets lend themselves to the matrix approach required for laying out periods of time on one axis and cash flow data on the other axis. In this way, information in any cell can be subjected to arithmetical and discount calculations.

The more substantial a project is, relative to the size of the firm, the more sifting should be done before approval is given. We are now going to examine various approaches to risk and uncertainty ranging from a crude payback criterion at one extreme to portfolio theory at the other.

Payback method

Payback was described in a previous chapter as a relatively crude technique used to test the viability of projects. This is performed by counting the number of years it takes to recover the original investment using either undiscounted or discounted cash flows.

Sometimes firms use payback in a slightly different context to reduce the risk element in a project by setting a maximum allowable payback period. When this is applied to cash flows discounted at the firm's cost of capital, it ensures that the minimum required return is always achieved and that cash is quickly generated for reinvestment in a new project.

EXAMPLE 9.1

Comparison of two projects by payback criterion

Year	Project A	Project B
	£	£
0	−10,000	−10,000
1	+4,000	0
2	+4,000	+4,000
3	+4,000	+4,000
4	+4,000	+4,000
5	0	+4,000
6	0	+4,000
7	0	+4,000
8	0	+4,000
Payback period	2.5 years	3.5 years
DCF yield	22%	25%

If the maximum payback period was set at three years then Project A would be selected rather than the more profitable, but slow starting, Project B.

If we can assume that events in the coming year or two are more capable of being forecast with a high degree of certainty then it also reduces the risk element. This is because distant cash flows are multiplied by relatively small present value factors and, conversely, a higher weighting is given to more immediate cash flows.

These advantages are sufficient for many firms, and payback remains one of the most popular appraisal techniques. We should be aware, however, of its potential weakness in selecting less profitable projects by its concentration on quick returns.

Pessimistic and optimistic forecasts

Instead of pinning all their faith on the DCF yield resulting from the expected cash flows, firms sometimes calculate two further sets of cash flows based on pessimistic and optimistic assumptions respectively.

At one extreme will be the combination of the pessimistic assumptions. This will assume highest capital cost, shortest life, lowest sales volume and price, highest operating cost and the like. The DCF yield prepared from this data will be the lowest return envisaged.

At the other extreme will be the cash flows resulting from everything being favourable at the same time. This situation will incorporate the lowest possible capital cost, longest life, highest sales volume and price, lowest running cost and so on. The resultant DCF yield will be the highest possible return that could be achieved.

In effect the pessimistic and optimistic forecasts set the outer limits, or parameters, within which we would expect to find the actual DCF yield. They therefore give a better perspective of the range within which the return on investment will fall.

If either of the two extreme conditions are very unlikely to occur, managers should not pay them too much attention in their decision-taking. The main drawback of this method is now apparent. It does not quantify the degree of optimism or pessimism assumed in the sets of cash flows.

EXAMPLE 9.2

DCF yields on different sets of cash flows

	Pessimistic(%)	*Expected(%)*	*Optimistic(%)*
Project A	22	27	40
Project B	−12	12	21
Project C	− 3	20	40

If this company required a return of say 20 per cent, then Project A will be approved as it satisfies the 20 per cent required return in all conceivable circumstance. It is very unlikely Project B will be approved, however, as only in the most optimistic circumstances will the 20 per cent criterion just be satisfied. Project C is more difficult to evaluate as the possibility of a small loss has to be balanced against the possibility of a very high rate of return of 40 per cent.

Probability theory

A statistical technique that can be applied to overcome this weakness is contained in probability theory.

EXAMPLE 9.3

A firm is considering buying new equipment costing £80,000 which has an expected life of ten years and is also expected to save £17,600 in operating costs each year when compared with existing methods. It is thought that at worst these savings would not fall below £11,600 per annum and at best that they would not exceed £23,600 per annum. The project manager has assigned subjective probability factors to various estimates of savings which are used to calculate the expected or weighted average DCF yield:

Annual saving	*Probability factor*	*DCF yield(%)*	*DCF yield x probability(%)*
£11,600	.05	7	0.35
£13,600	.15	11	1.65
£15,600	.25	15	3.75
£17,600	.33	18	5.94
£19,600	.15	21	3.15
£21,600	.05	24	1.20
£23,600	.02	27	0.54
	1.00		16.58

The weighted average or expected DCF yield turns out to be 16.6 per cent which would be satisfactory if the required return was set at a lower level. If the required return was, say, 20 per cent this project would not be satisfactory as the expected DCF yield at 16.6 per cent is significantly less. Only the last three sets of possible cash flows yield a return in excess of 20 per cent and their combined probabilities or level of confidence in a satisfactory outcome is only 0.22, which is 22 per cent.

On a more complex project, like an expansion scheme to sell a new product, we can apply probability factors to each constituent item making up the cash flows. In this case we would use computers to perform the hundreds of reiterative calculations and there are appropriate programs dedicated to this task.

Decision trees

Sometimes managers are faced with a choice between alternative courses of action with the possibility of further alternative courses of action in later years depending on which original choice was made.

A technique known as a 'decision tree' is used to set out all possible alternatives and to show the further alternatives they lead to in future years. The analogy with a tree comes from the nodes and branches. At each node there is a choice of branches. Each branch leads to a further node at which another choice of branches is made, and so on until all possible outcomes are exhausted.

If the nodes represent decision points for investment and the branches are quantified for the benefits gained, we can attach probability factors to each branch to quantify the expected monetary value of each alternative event. Managers should therefore choose the path which maximises this money benefit.

EXAMPLE 9.4

A manager of a research department is considering what to do about an ongoing project. He can either abandon it, keep the expenditure at the same level, or increase it substantially to improve the likelihood of success. Abandoning will result in costs of £20,000; maintaining the present level of activity will cost £50,000; doubling the present effort to improve the chances of success will cost £100,000. By the end of the year it will be known whether the project has succeeded or failed. Failure brings no further costs with it, whilst success would result in the sale of know-how for £300,000.

At the present level of research activity the success/failure ratio is put at 40 per cent/60 per cent but the enhanced effort would improve the prospects to about 80 per cent/20 per cent.

All the above information can be expressed graphically in the form of a decision tree as shown in Figure 9.1 and the gains/losses from the various outcomes evaluated.

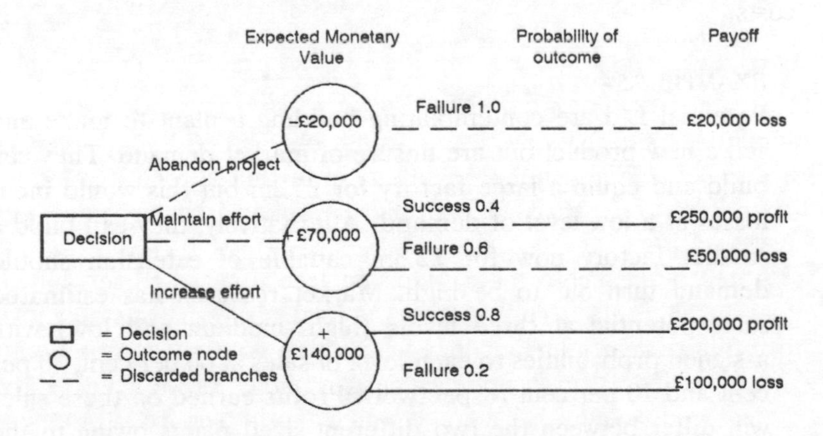

Figure 9.1 *Decision tree of alternative research strategies*

In this example the three alternative courses of action are valued by netting off the probable gain against its respective cost. Taking the alternative to increase the research effort as an example, the expected monetary value of £140,000 = (0.8 x £200,000) – (0.2 x £100,000). This expected monetary value is the highest of the three alternatives and is therefore the preferred solution.

This solution may still not be acceptable to some firms. There is a 20 per cent chance of failure on the recommended course of action which has been allowed for in the probability factors. For a large firm with many projects this may be acceptable as the risk/reward ratio is very satisfactory. In a small firm the failure of this one project, out of a small total, may be catastrophic.

1. Incorporating present values. The above illustration of a decision tree did not include any subsequent decisions. Also, because of the short time-span of only one year, the present value of money was ignored. It is when dealing with more complex situations that decision trees are most useful. They do not bring new information to bear on the decision but set it out in the most helpful way.

The points in time at which decisions have to be made are clearly identified along with the different possible outcomes evaluated in money and probability terms. This enables the decision-making manager to choose the most desirable course of action based on the net present value of the weighted benefits less costs.

EXAMPLE 9.5

Potential Ltd are contemplating building a plant to make and sell a new product but are unsure of market demand. They can build and equip a large factory for £5.2m but this would incur losses at a low level of demand. Alternatively, they can build a smaller factory now for £2.8m capable of extension should demand turn out to be high. Market research has estimated sales potential at three levels (high, medium and low) with assigned probabilities to each level of sales at 60 per cent, 30 per cent and 10 per cent respectively. Profits earned on these sales will differ between the two different-sized plants owing to the inability of the small plant to meet the high level of sales (without expansion) and the uneconomic operation of the large plant at the low level of sales. The expected annual profits before depreciation charges for the next eight years are:

	Large plant	*Small plant*
High demand	£2.0m	£0.9m
Medium demand	£1.0m	£0.7m
Low demand	(£0.4m)	£0.5m

Assuming the small plant was constructed it will be able to cope with the low and medium levels of demand. If the high level of sales materialises it will be possible to extend the small plant at the end of Year 2 for a cost of £2.6m after which annual profits will roughly equal those earned on the large plant.

These alternative courses of action and their net present value at the required rate of 20 per cent can be represented on a decision tree as in Figure 9.2.

When interpreting a decision tree we start at the extreme right-hand branches. The payoffs are 'rolled back' to the previous decision point where a choice between alternatives takes place. Intermediate payoffs are rolled back to their previous decision point until one eventually reaches the original decision point. This first decision is dependent on which route through the branches maximises the net present value benefit. In complex situations many decision points exist and the tree diagrams are quite involved, unlike Figure 9.2 which only includes two decision points.

In that example the second decision concerns the choice whether to expand the small-scale plant after two years or not. On the current forecasts of demand and the likelihood of occurrence it does not appear worthwhile. The NPV surplus of £1.57m is less than the £1.85m obtained from running the small plant at its original size for a further six years. This preferred solution rolls back to influence the original decision to build the small plant because the NPV surplus of £0.88m exceeds the £0.40m surplus obtained from building the large plant.

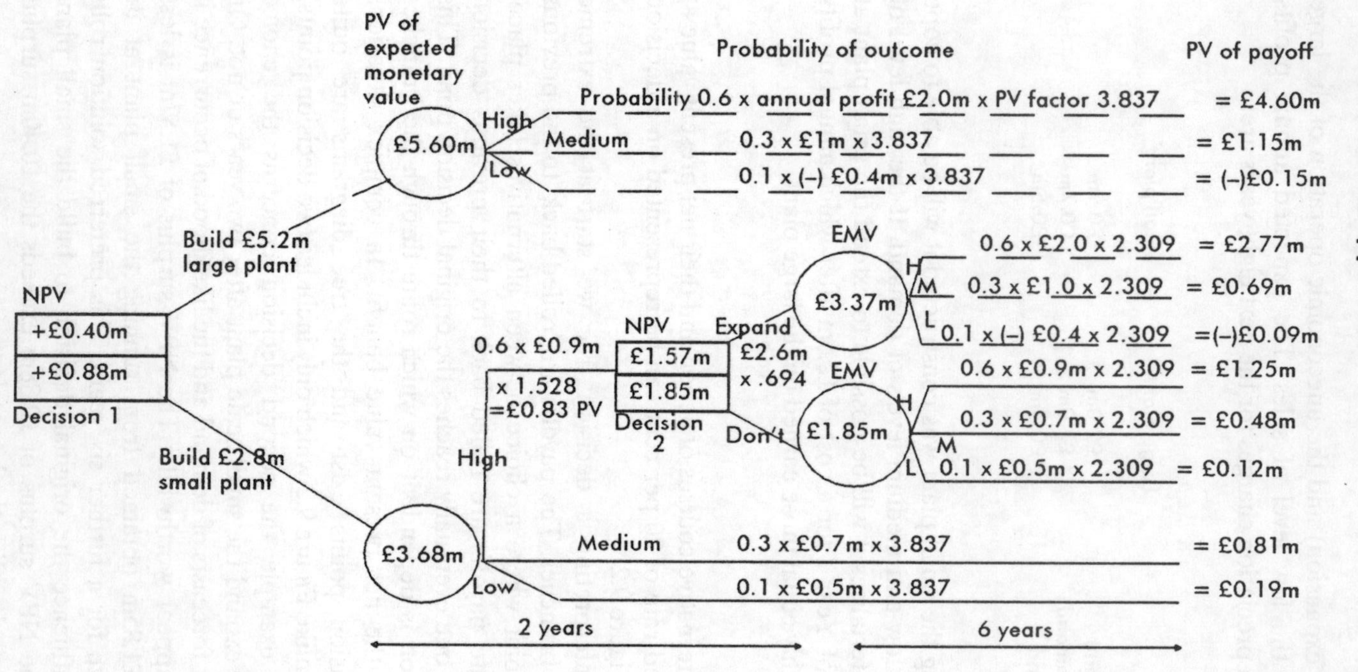

Figure 9.2 *Decision tree of expansion project*

Risk premium

Another approach to risk is to recognise that different kinds of investment carry different degrees of risk and should therefore be set different target rates of return. A simple approach to this idea is to add an extra discount rate, called a 'risk premium', to the basic cost of capital, so setting different target rates of return for different risk categories of investment. The risk premium may vary according to the risk category of the investment under review and is based on a subjective assessment of the risks involved as the following example illustrates:

EXAMPLE 9.6

Risk category	*Type of project*	*Cost of capital (%)*	*Risk premium (%)*	*Target rate of return(%)*
No risk	Financing decision	15	–	15
Low risk	Cost saving — existing technology	15	3	18
Medium risk	Expansion — new markets, existing technology	15	10	25
High risk	Expansion — new markets, new technology	15	20	35

In practice investors demand a higher return on more risky investments than on less risky ones. By using the risk-premium approach firms are giving recognition in their individual investment appraisals to what investors themselves practise when investing in individual companies.

Portfolio theory

An extension of this idea is found in what is referred to as 'portfolio theory' where a collection of investments is described as a portfolio. Many portfolios can be constructed from different combinations of investments.

The risk level of each portfolio is measured by the variability of possible returns about the mean, expressed in standard deviations. Investors' attitudes to 'risk versus return' can be expressed on indifference curves. In Figure 9.3 any point on indifference curve IC1 gives a higher return, or lower risk, than its equivalent point on IC2, which itself is preferred to IC3.

When we add various alternative portfolios assigned the letters A-H on the same graph, the selected portfolio will be the one which reaches the highest possible indifference curve. This is indicated on Figure 9.3 as portfolio E which is the closest to IC2, with no portfolio reaching IC1.

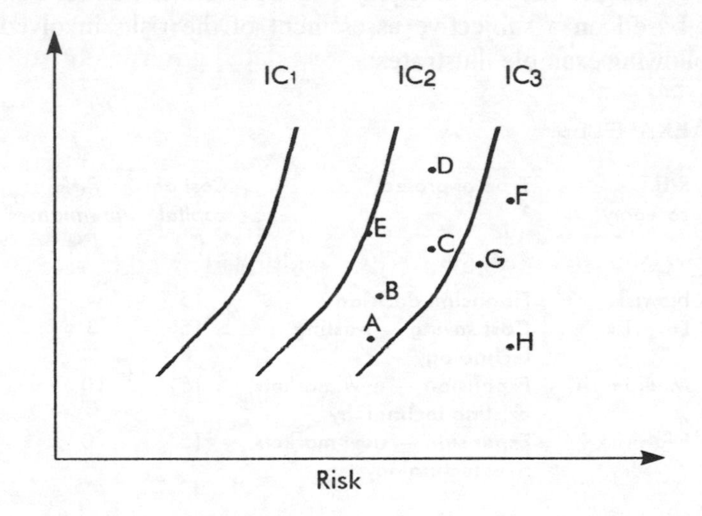

Figure 9.3 *Portfolio selection*

Portfolio theory goes on to say that it is not the individual project risk that matters but its effect on the overall portfolio's risk. Therefore when we evaluate a risky project we need to correlate the individual project risk to that of the existing portfolio it would join if accepted.

2. Capital asset pricing model. A branch of portfolio theory called the 'Capital Asset Pricing Model' states that we should calculate the net present value on a new project at a composite discount rate comprising:

(*a*) a rate of interest representing the risk free cost of capital plus (*b*) a risk premium or discount determined by the correlation of the risk on the individual project to the risk on the whole existing portfolio it would join. The size of this correlation is referred to as the beta factor and can vary from –1.0 to + 1.0.

EXAMPLE 9.7

XYZ Ltd have an existing portfolio of capital investments yielding an expected return of 20 per cent. They are considering a new project with an expected yield of 15 per cent. The beta factor for this new project has been calculated at 0.42. The current risk free return on long-dated government stocks is 11 per cent.

Instead of taking a weighted average cost of capital as the criterion for judging this new project, the CAPM approach uses a discount rate composed of the risk-free cost of capital plus the portfolio risk premium when multiplied by the beta factor as follows:

Risk free rate	=	11%
Risk premium	=	portfolio return — risk free rate
	=	20% – 11% = 9%
Beta factor	=	0.42

Required rate of return is therefore 14.8% comprising

the Risk free rate	+	(Risk premium	x	Beta factor)	
11%	+ (	9%	x	0.42	)

The above project is therefore very marginal with an expected yield of 15 per cent just equalling its required discount rate of 14.8 per cent. The ideal situation is for firms to find new investment opportunities with such different risk characteristics to the existing portfolio that it results in a negative beta factor. This may be easier in practice with investments in financial securities than with industrial/commercial investments.

Sensitivity analysis

One further approach to risk in the context of investment appraisal is that of sensitivity testing. This takes the form of recalculating the NPV or DCF yield assuming a different value for any one variable in the cash flows.

EXAMPLE 9.8

A firm requires a minimum real return of 15 per cent on any new investment and is proposing to buy a new machine costing £20,000 which is expected to save £5,000 each year of its ten-year life. This project may be sensitive to any reduction in the expected life or annual saving.

First the DCF yield is calculated on the expected events which turns out to be 21 per cent. Next an arbitrary percentage change in one variable is taken and the DCF yield recalculated to get an estimate of sensitivity. If, say, the estimated life was 10 per cent less at only nine years, the DCF yield is still as high as 20 per cent and therefore this project is relatively insensitive to variations in the length of life. This would not be true, however, in the case of short-life projects of only a few years.

A variation on this sensitivity test is to calculate the minimum number of years life needed to yield the required 15 per cent return. Holding the savings variable constant at £5,000 p.a. on the £20,000 investment we find:

Life (yrs)	*DCF yield*
10	21%
9	20%
8	18%
7	16%
6	13%

We can therefore conclude that the investment is viable if the life expectancy is seven years or more.

The sensitivity test is then repeated for a 10 per cent reduction in the annual savings reverting to the original expected life of ten years. This reduces the DCF yield from the original 21 per cent to only 18 per cent, so we conclude that this project is more sensitive to inaccuracies in the savings estimate than to those in its estimated life.

The minimum savings value needed for the project to be viable over its ten year life can also be evaluated at just under £4,000 p.a.

Many other techniques are available to deal with risk being an area of most concern in the investment decision and one much favoured by academics. As mentioned earlier, the use of dedicated programs or computer spreadsheets are invaluable for this kind of treatment of the cash flows.

Summary

It is unrealistic to assume that there will be one certain set of net cash flows on a project apart from exceptional cases. The consequences of different values of cash flows being possible means we should allow for this when assessing the profitability of an investment. Relatively crude techniques like payback, risk premium and optimistic/pessimistic forecasts can be used, but projects absorbing a significant amount of a firm's capital demand more sophisticated treatment.

The DCF yield or NPV methods can both be used to test how sensitive they are to variations in any one key variable in the cash flows. Having identified the items of cash flow which are most significant, these can be given maximum management attention at both the design and operation stages. They also assume importance for the post audit mentioned in the concluding chapter.

An alternative, or perhaps additional, technique is to construct various sets of net cash flows based on different assumptions. The likelihood of each occurring is subjectively assessed and a probability factor allocated accordingly. The profitability of a project can now be assessed as a weighted average of all the possible events.

In case this sounds like too much work the existence of computer programs reduces the analysis to a matter of minutes at most. The compilation of the cash flows and the assignment of probability factors will obviously take much longer but will be time well spent compared to the consequences of a bad decision.

A further approach is based on portfolio theory taking the view that an investment should not be regarded in isolation but as an addition to existing investments. When the risk category of the new investment differs from that of the existing portfolio this affects the required return used in the discounting process.

We should be aware that within this scientific approach there is still a place for management art and subjective judgement. When these are reinforced by a quantitative assessment of the costs and benefits, as described above, then the outcome is surely improved. We must guard against the possible danger of being mesmerised by a numerical answer of great mathematical precision built on weak foundations.

Progress test 9

1. What are the advantages and disadvantages of using a payback method to allow for risk and uncertainty?
2. 'Setting parameters in the optimistic/pessimistic forecast approach to risk and uncertainty is unrealistic because the combination of events contained in either parameter is so unlikely to happen'. Discuss.
3. How can the weakness, hinted at in Question 2, be overcome?
4. Describe some situations in which decision trees could be helpful to a decision maker.
5. Can one find a list of 'risk premiums' to apply to various categories of investment for use by any company? Give reasons for your answer.
6. 'Portfolio theory sounds fine for financial investment in stocks and shares, but can the ideas be related to industrial and commercial investment projects?'
7. Explain the various kinds of sensitivity tests which could be performed on an investment in word processing equipment to reduce typists' labour costs.

10

Life-cycle costing

Principles of life-cycle costing

Life-cycle costing is a relatively new concept which attempts to optimise the cost of physical assets over their whole life. The choice of buildings or plant is often based solely on original capital costs without regard to subsequent operating costs, maintenance costs or replacement intervals.

The philosophy behind life-cycle costing is that it brings together all the costs of ownership and operation over the whole life of an asset, using the present value technique. It can therefore be used to evaluate trade-off situations, for example between a higher initial cost to save on future running costs, or between one asset and another asset with different cost characteristics.

You will all have seen the following kind of advertisement: 'This washing machine is easily the cheapest on the market. It won't last!' The unintentional double meaning speaks volumes for the need to look at the total costs of the washing machine over its whole life, rather than just concentrate on the initial acquisition cost.

In other words it is important to realise that the lowest purchase cost is not necessarily the lowest overall cost over the whole life of the asset. Higher maintenance costs and a shorter life may outweigh the higher acquisition cost of an alternative washing machine.

Most firms normally keep a record of assets acquired and somewhere else in their costing system keep details of the operating and maintenance costs of these same assets. What very few firms do is to put all this information together to monitor the cost of owning and using assets over their whole life. In other words, few firms practice what is called 'life-cycle costing'.

This technique calls for the prediction of expected life-cycle costs (LCC) for management decision-making purposes, and the monitoring of actual LCC to modify decisions previously made and to provide data for future decisions.

It is therefore concerned with predicting future LCC by the feedforward of information about the expected performance which can later be corrected by feedback of information on actual performance. The justification for attempting this monitoring process is that it could result in a substantial saving in costs over the total life of an asset. Any saving in costs must result in increased profits.

1. **Terotechnology**. The concept of terotechnology embraces this idea of life-cycle costing. Terotechnology is defined as 'a combination of management, financial, engineering and other practices applied to physical assets in pursuit of economic life-cycle costs'. It is concerned with designing for the reliability and maintainability of physical assests together with the economy of their installation, commissioning, operation and eventual disposal.

The physical asset can be a building, an item of plant, a ship, a vehicle, an oil rig or even a whole configuration of plant. The idea of terotechnology may be new but the practices and techniques it embodies are already in use but not necessarily combined together to try to optimise the cost of using physical assets over their whole life. Life-cycle costing is really the financial arm of terotechnology.

Life-cycle stages and costs

A typical life-cycle will straddle a number of company accounting periods starting with the specification and design of the asset through the sequential stages of its life to its eventual disposal. The life-cycle need not be the complete life of the asset if the user intends to dispose of it before it is worn out, or, in the case of a building, alter its use after a certain time.

Usually some LCC start with the maker (to be later reimbursed by the purchaser) whilst the remaining LCC commence with the user. The main stages of the LCC of any physical asset can be described as shown in Figure 10.1.

Taking a photocopying machine as an example, the LCC for the user will comprise the original acquisition cost (including specification, design and manufacture of the photocopier) plus the annual operating and maintenance costs over its total life. These annual costs will include the costs of paper, energy, operator's time and maintenance.

Because these LCC occur in different years we need to bring them to a common point of time by using the now familiar present value concept. When considering actual LCC we must use suitable published indices of labour and material costs, to bring them to Year 0 value £s by inflating previous years' figures by the percentage movement in that index.

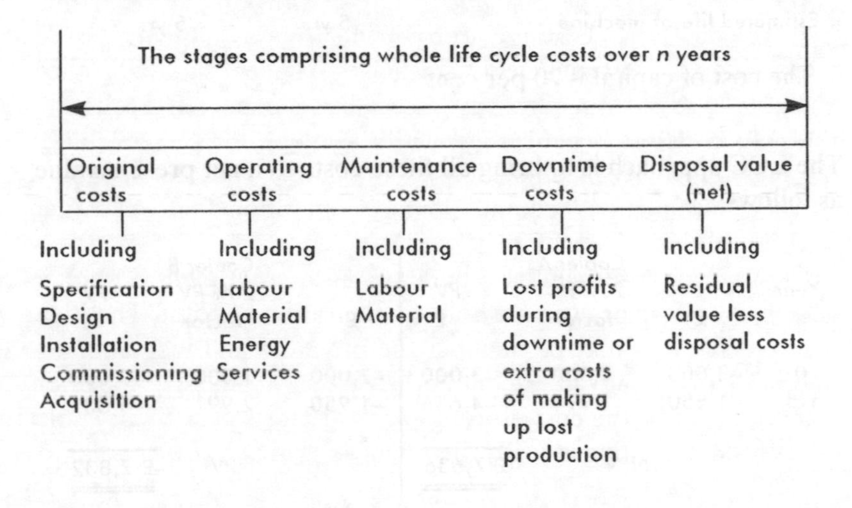

Figure 10.1 *Typical life cycle costs*

2. Choice decisions. One very valuable use of this life-cycle costing approach is when evaluating alternative machines at the acquisition stage. Very often the advantages of one machine are offset by its disadvantages when compared with an alternative machine of different design. These advantages and disadvantages will probably not be equal and 'trade-off' studies are required to determine the best buy.

EXAMPLE 10.1

A firm is trying to choose between two alternative models of a photocopying machine with the following costs:

	Copier A	Copier B
	£	£
Acquisition and installation cost	3,000	2,000
Annual costs: maintenance contract	200	300
paper	350	400
operator's salary (part)	1,000	1,250
	1,550	1,950
Estimated life of machine	5 yrs	5 yrs

The cost of capital is 20 per cent.

The LCC approach is to bring all these costs to a net present value as follows:

Year	£	Copier A 20% PV factor	PV £	£	Copier B 20% PV factor	PV £
0	–3,000	1.000	–3,000	–2,000	1.000	–2,000
1-5	–1,550	2.991	–4,636	–1,950	2.991	–5,832
		NPV	–£ 7,636		NPV	–£ 7,832

We can conclude from its lower NPV cost that the higher initial cost of plain paper Copier A is more than offset by the savings on operating speed, lower maintenance cost and cheaper paper when compared with Copier B which uses specialised paper.

Copier A is cheaper over its whole life-cycle because the extra £1,000 purchase price is more than offset by the savings of £400 p.a. in running costs in each of the next five years. A return of £400 p.a. on an incremental investment of £1,000 is equivalent to a DCF yield of 29 per cent. This more than satisfies the 20 per cent cost of capital assumed in the above example.

The lowest LCC in present value terms will always denote the most attractive asset from a range of alternatives provided the asset fulfils its operational requirements adequately.

It is important to compare alternatives on a 'like with like' basis. In the case of the photocopiers, both alternative machines had the same life expectancy of five years. If this had not been the case the present value LCC for each alternative could be calculated from the number of years which represents the lowest common denominator of all the alternative's lives. This lowest common denominator may include a number of repetitive life-cycles for any one asset thereby requiring periodic asset replacements to be included in the computations.

Costs-in-use/annual equivalent cost

A more attractive approach when comparing the LCC of assets with different lives is to express both the initial purchase and subsequent running costs on an annual basis. In certain industries this approach is called 'costs-in-use' and in others it is referred to as the annual equivalent cost.

Operating costs are already expressed on an annual basis so we need to examine how the initial purchase cost is expressed as an equal annual cost. We do this by finding what amounts to a mortgage repayment for the capital cost including interest at the firm's cost of capital.

The calculation is performed by dividing the capital cost by the relevant cumulative PV factor for the specified life and rate of interest.

EXAMPLE 10.2

In the case of Copier A the purchase cost of £3,000 is divided by the five-year cumulative PV factor at 20 per cent (2.991) to give an annual equivalent cost of £1,003.

$$\text{Annual equivalent cost} = \frac{\text{Purchase cost}}{\text{Cum PV factor}}$$

$$= \frac{£3{,}000}{2.991} = £1{,}003 \text{ p.a.}$$

We then add the yearly operating cost of £1,550 to find the total costs-in-use as follows:

Copier A	£
Annual equivalent cost of copier	1,003
Annual operating costs	1,550
Costs-in-use	£2,553

This annual cost could then be compared with the costs-in-use of other copiers expected to last, say, six years and four years respectively. The comparison is valid because the costs being compared relate to the same length of time (one year) in each case.

It is implicit in this example comparing the LCC of alternative copiers that the value (and quality) of the output is the same. If the income generated by alternative assets is not identical then this must be taken into account when comparing their LCC.

This could be done by comparing income and costs in the present value calculations over the whole life of the asset. Alternatively, the extra or incremental income of one asset could be netted off against its yearly running costs when comparing the LCC of competing assets.

Applications of LCC technique

Every year numerous purchases of buildings and equipment are based on the acquisition cost alone. Purchasing officers and other managers may be beguiled by a seemingly attractive acquisition cost for which 'benefit' their firms will pay in later years through high running costs or a short life. Lowest purchase price does not necessarily minimise total cost over the whole life of the asset and therefore does not maximise profits.

If managers have to make decisions on the acquisition of new plant or buildings with sparse information on past or expected performance and costs, then this cannot lead to the best choice. The consequence may be high operating and maintenance costs, excessive downtime, and wasted effort throughout the organisation, which could have been channelled to better use.

This idea of LCC is little more than applied common sense. It is the approach some people take in their personal lives when weighing up the merits of consumer durables, like cars. Although we may not carry out precise calculations we are intuitively influenced by differences in expected lives, the cost and frequency of services, fuel consumption and the like. Managers should apply this same approach in their business lives to any proposed purchase of a physical asset, be it a building, a machine, a vehicle, an aeroplane or anything else.

All firms in either the public or private sectors can apply LCC to the physical assets they use. These physical assets are alternatively called 'fixed assets' and, money spent on acquiring them is called 'capital expenditure'.

In central government these physical assets will include, for example, warships and hospitals; in local government LCC can be applied to council houses and leisure pools; in manufacturing industry relevant assets will include the buildings, plant, equipment and vehicles used in the production process; whilst service industries can apply these principles to the buildings, computers and other assets essential to provide a particular service to their clients. LCC can also be applied to consumer durable goods like motor cars and washing machines.

3. Parties involved in LCC. There are two parties interested in the LCC of an asset – the maker and the user. These two parties may occasionally be the same as in the case of a builder constructing an office block for his own use, or an engineering firm designing and making a machine for use in their own works. The different approaches of these two parties can perhaps be illustrated by looking at the LCC of a car.

As car owners we have all bemoaned the lack of really adequate anti-corrosion treatment of car bodies at the manufacturing stage. Technological improvements have greatly extended the life of the mechanical parts of a car but thinner panels and salty roads have reduced the average length of the life of the car body and hence the life of the car. For relatively little extra cost, some anti-corrosion treatment or the use of alternative metals in the manufacturing process could greatly extend the life of a car.

Why then do manufacturers not oblige? They will probably say that the customer is looking for the lowest possible initial cost.

Because manufacturers are competing on price in a highly competitive market, one manufacturer will not risk pricing himself out of that market for an intangible benefit the buyer cannot always immediately see.

In this age of high labour and energy costs motorists are coming round to thinking in terms of the LCC of their car rather than just its initial cost or visual appeal. The high costs of petrol and servicing are making buyers more conscious of these subsequent costs so they no longer plump for the lowest initial price of a particular range of cars.

This greater awareness by users is leading manufacturers to examine the design specification of their cars to reduce mud traps, to protect the most vulnerable panels and sections and to design bodies and engines to minimise petrol consumption and reduce service or repair costs. An example of this approach in the late 1970s was by Ford when they introduced their Fiesta model to the market.

In this way manufacturers are applying LCC principles to car production by looking at users future costs and not designing solely to minimise production costs. The resulting design may not be the cheapest design they can produce, but the user's total costs over the whole life of the car will be reduced.

Users, therefore, should be prepared to pay an extra initial cost commensurate with these expected future benefits. It should not be assumed, however, that the application of terotechnology will always lead to a greater initial capital cost.

Cost codes

An industrial application of life-cycle costing would be to collate the costs of ownership and use of a physical asset, or even a configuration or group of assets. The source of all costing information is the document which originally records the transaction. Typical documents are time-cards, stores issue notes and invoices. Accountants use a shorthand system called a 'cost code' to describe the nature of transactions.

The cost code is constructed in sections with each section having a specific purpose. For example, blocks of numbers or letters may be used to describe the kind of expense or work carried out, which department did the work, who it was done for and possibly which physical asset was used. Use of cost codes allows a description of the transaction and its value to be fed into computer systems. There it is sorted and stored until retrieved at a later date to provide valuable information. Example 10.3 illustrates this approach

EXAMPLE 10.3

2 7	5 6 4	8 3 7 2	1 0 6
Location or dept. number	Description of expense, work done	Job, product or project number	Physical asset number

By including a physical asset number in the cost code, all the LCC of acquisition, installation, commissioning, operation, maintenance and disposal can be logged against that particular asset. Although LCC is a relatively simple idea it needs careful thought and planning to realise the potential benefits of its application.

4. Information flows. Both manufacturers and users of physical assets can make use of LCC data. Manufacturers should try to get feedback of users's cost data regarding the performance of their equipment. This is the main source of information on the LCC of their products which will encourage them to modify existing models or completely redesign the next generation of equipment or buildings.

Ideally there should be a flow of cost and technical data through the sequential stages of a life-cycle. There needs to be a flow of LCC information to allow appraisals to be carried out on modifications, trade-offs and replacement decisions. Costs at one stage of the life-cycle are influenced by decisions made at previous stages of the life-cycle and hence a feedback of information to those stages is also important. This process may involve both manufacturer and user as the diagram in Figure 10.2 portrays.

The feedback of information from user to manufacturer may not always take place. This may particularly occur when the physical assets concerned are of relatively low value and used singly by

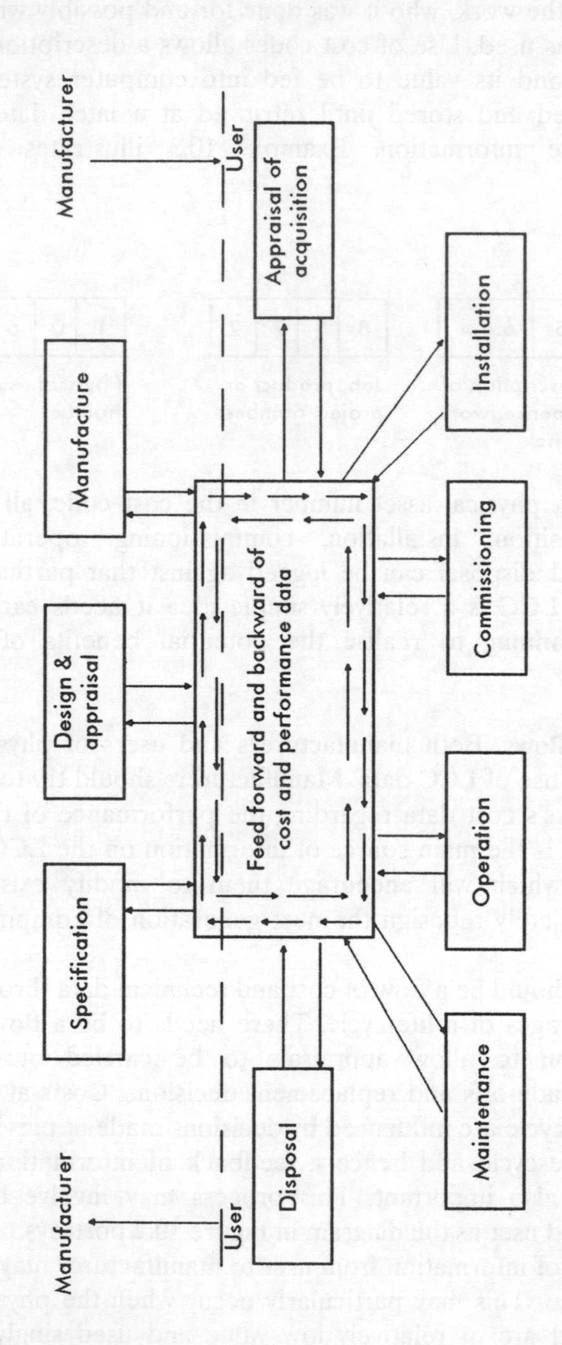

Figure 10.2 *Flow of cost and technical information*

many firms. In this situation individual users may not each collect the necessary cost and performance data to feed back to the manufacturers' designers, as it would not seem worth the user's costs of collection.

Faced with this lack of direct feedback, manufacturers can attempt to keep contact with users through their technical representatives. Additionally they can give incentives to users to record data by guaranteeing a certain standard of reliability. They can also offer 'post design' services to rectify faults or modify equipment as necessary. Examples already exist of manufacturers quoting specifications for their equipment in LCC terms.

5. User benefits. The other party who can make good use of data on LCC terms is the user himself. The following four ways summarise how users can benefit from thinking in life-cycle terms.

Pre-design stage.

At the pre-design stage users should consider terotechnological aspects of the design before passing the specification to their chosen manufacturer. This approach will consider the reliability and maintainability of the physical asset in LCC terms and examine trade-offs between capital and operating or maintenance costs. In some cases the application of terotechnology may even lead to lower capital and operating costs than had previously been experienced with similar assets.

A common occurrence in the design of new buildings is when the user's architect considers various trade-offs.

EXAMPLE 10.4

A simple illustration is whether to specify metal-framed windows needing minimal maintenance and having a long life expectancy or, alternatively, to specify wooden-framed windows with more frequent maintenance needs and a shorter life. The extra capital cost of the metal windows trade-off against its lower maintenance costs and less frequent replacement when compared with the initially cheaper wooden frames.

Possible trade-offs at the pre-design stage are between:

(*a*) capital cost
(*b*) operating cost
(*c*) maintenance cost
(*d*) trade-in or disposal value

The examination of these trade-offs may have to be based on estimated values in cases where more accurate data is not available. Nevertheless an attempt should be made to consider the long-term cost consequences of aspects of design.

Acquisition stage.
Another use of the LCC concept occurs at the acquisition stage. Here users may have a choice of alternative physical assets offered either by the same manufacturer or by his competitors. Consideration of the expected costs at all stages of the life-cycle for each model should ensure the best buy.

EXAMPLE 10.5
A situation was discussed earlier in this chapter when the LCC of two photocopiers were compared. In that case the initially dearer copier A turned out to be the better buy when compared on an LCC basis with the alternative copier B. This was because the extra initial cost of copier A was more than offset by the benefit of lower operating and maintenance costs over its whole life.

Usage stage.
The monitoring of actual LCC against the budgeted or predicted LCC may highlight the desirability of modifications in service. This does not mean that users have to wait until the end of an asset's life to make such comparisons.

If budgeted LCC are broken down into shorter periods, or cost horizons, then more frequent comparisons of budgeted with actual LCC can be made.

EXAMPLE 10.6

An example of this approach is contained in Case Study No. 6 in Appendix 1. This describes a brewery bottling plant where it was found that much higher losses of beer occurred than had been allowed for in the life-cycle budget. Engineering studies to trace the malfunction led to a modification by the brewery. Information fed back to the manufacturer also led to a redesign of this machine for the benefit of subsequent users.

It is possible and beneficial to break into the life-cycle at any stage even if a life-cycle budget was not prepared before acquisition. For example, it may be possible to design out high maintenance costs or costs of downtime.

Replacement stage.

Where a user owns a number of similar physical assets and records their LCC he has a valuable source of information to help him decide when to replace such assets. The greater the sample of physical assets then the more representative and statistically reliable will be the life-cycle costs. In effect this is another trade-off situation where the higher costs of using and maintaining a physical asset for a further period of time are offset by delaying the cost of a replacement.

EXAMPLE 10.7

An example of the approach is contained in Case Study No. 7 in Appendix 1. For the moment let us assume we have been able to calculate the LCC of a physical asset for the same period of years, first assuming the machine is replaced every year, then every two years, every three years and every four years. The present values of these LCC are £75,000, £68,000, £64,000 and £69,000 respectively.

When we plot the LCC against the replacement interval on a graph the result is shown as Figure 10.3.

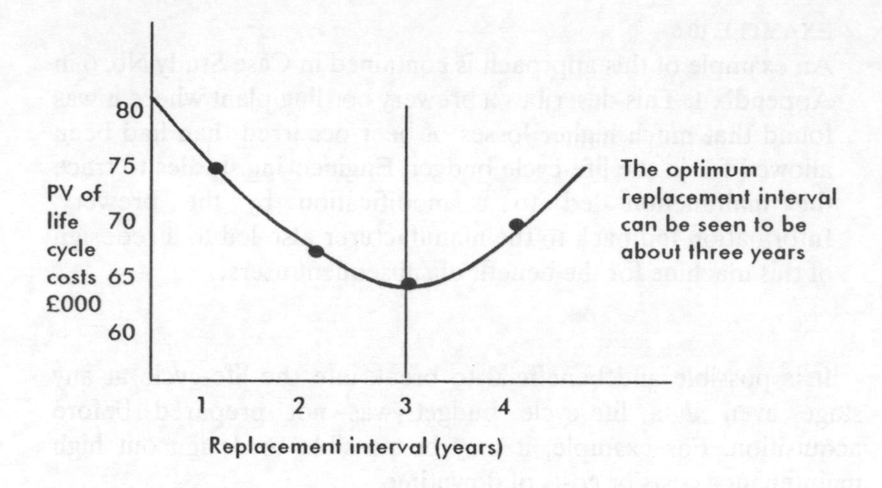

Figure 10.3 *Comparison of LCC at varying replacement intervals*

Summary

This chapter aims to encourage both manufacturers and users of physical assets to think in life-cycle cost terms. Increasing competition in world markets should encourage manufacturers to consider all aspects of the assets they create. The concepts of terotechnology and life-cycle costing have an important contribution to make in achieving cost-effective designs.

Users should be aware that LCC may be many times more than the original capital cost. Unless attention is paid to subsequent stages of the life-cycle a cheap acquisition may prove to be very expensive. Firms should choose physical assets on the basis of predicted LCC and monitor actual LCC to highlight necessary design modifications.

Progress test 10

1. What is the broad aim and purpose of life-cycle costing?
2. Calculate the annual equivalent cost (or costs-in-use) of a motor vehicle, given the following data:

Purchase cost	£20,000
Expected life	5 years
Scrap value at end	£500
Maintenance costs	£2,000 p.a.
Tax, insurance etc.	£2,500 p.a.
Cost of capital	15%

3. Compare and contrast the basic structure of the cost code in Example 10.3 with that of your own organisation.
4. What are the specific uses to which
(*a*) the manufacturer
(*b*) the user
of a physical asset can put LCC data.

11

Cost-benefit analysis

This might seem to be a surprising chapter title to include at this stage of the book, when the whole essence of investment appraisal contained in previous chapters has been the weighing up of costs against benefits.

The term 'cost–benefit analysis' is sometimes used in a broad way to describe the appraisal of say, a proposed new product, or a cost-saving investment. Such cases examine the costs and benefits as they accrue to the one investing party. They identify the capital and running costs of the investment and relate the yearly benefits to those costs in terms of an NPV or DCF yield.

Definition

There are other investment situations, particularly investments by public sector organisations, where it is not adequate to examine costs and benefits from the narrow viewpoint of the investing party. This is because other costs and/or benefits are borne by other interested parties, for example the wider community, or different public bodies, or private sector firms. Such costs or benefits affecting parties other than the investing party making the decision are known as 'social costs' and 'social benefits'.

'Cost–benefit analysis' (CBA) is the term used to describe these wider investment appraisals of public sector investments, for example, new roads, bridges, tunnels, dams or airports. It is mainly applied to relatively large and expensive projects because of the time and expense involved in collecting and evaluating the data.

There are many famous CBA studies that have been carried out in the past including the M1 motorway (London–Birmingham section), the London Underground Victoria Line and the choice of site for a third London Airport. Not so famous, but very important to local communities and firms, may be city by-pass proposals or major road widening schemes.

Illustration

If we take as a simple example a local authority scheme to purchase some land, currently in agricultural use, and develop it as an industrial estate, the interested parties will probably include:

(*a*) the local authority initiating the development;
(*b*) adjoining local authorities;
(*c*) the vendor (farmer) of the land;
(*d*) agricultural employees of the vendor;
(*e*) the local community;
(*f*) incoming firms;
(*g*) new employees;
(*h*) central government.

1. Social costs and benefits. The social costs and benefits accruing to such a scheme now need identification and evaluation. It may not always be necessary to put values on costs and benefits if the net effect on each affected party points in the same direction. Examples of social costs and benefits for each party will include the following.

Local authority. The initiating local authority incurs the capital cost of clearing and preparing the site and installing main services. This capital cost will also include interest charges as the development may take a few years to complete. Benefits will include the sale of sites to incoming firms, possible grants from central government, increased rate income and a better use of other social capital if not already fully utilised.

When costs and benefits are aggregated for all parties, some costs to one party will cancel out benefits to another party and have no overall effect. For example, the government grants described as a benefit to the local authority is also an identical cost to central government. These transactions are known as 'transfer payments' and can be included at nil value because they cancel out overall.

Other local authorities. These may incur social capital costs on the provision of housing, etc., dependent on current usage of housing stock and whether relocation of new employees to the area takes place.

Vendor. The present occupier of the farm will incur the cost and inconvenience of moving to another farm bought with the proceeds of sale. This may or may not lead to a more profitable livelihood. More intangible and much more difficult to value is any feeling of loss if the farm has been passed down through generations.

Vendor's employees. The loss of their livelihood is a cost, but possible new employment on the industrial estate might outweigh such loss if industrial wages can be assumed to be higher than agricultural wages.

Local community. There are benefits through greater employment opportunities and the 'multiplier' effect of such an influx causing a knock-on demand for local retail and service industries. One possible cost may be the loss of amenity value particularly for people living near the proposed industrial site.

Incoming firms. There is a need for each firm to do its own investment appraisal of the costs and benefits of setting up on this site. Such costs and benefits will differ according to whether a firm is relocating from elsewhere by closing down previous premises, or expanding existing activities or simply starting up from scratch. In the more straightforward case of expansion, the capital costs of site acquisition and building new premises must be justified by the net income from the sale of goods or services.

New employees. Incoming firms will attract staff, whether currently employed or unemployed, only if they see a net benefit in income, or property values, or benefits in some other less quantifiable factor like the 'quality of life'.

Central government. The availability of grants or subsidies for developments in this area are a cost to central government. However, these initial costs may be offset by future savings on unemployment benefits if net new employment is created. There will also be the benefit of an increase in the taxation base for both direct and indirect taxes.

Comparison of CBA with investment appraisal

An economist working on the CBA of a public sector project is essentially asking the same question as does an accountant appraising a private sector investment. In both cases the question is whether the benefits exceed the costs over the life of the investment *after* the time value of money has been taken into account.

The difference in approach is that the economist asks the question on behalf of a much wider group of interested parties. The accountant in a private sector firm, however, is only concerned with costs incurred by, and benefits accruing to, the accountant's own organisation.

Although CBA is primarily a technique applied to proposed public sector investments, the recent blurring of the edges between public and private sectors in the late 1980s may make the technique more relevant to large civil engineering and construction firms.

Such firms, or a consortium of them, are now proposing various schemes to central government regarding new bridges, tunnels, roads and urban renewal. Consideration will have to be given to the wider social costs and benefits of many of these schemes and not just concentrate on those costs and benefits affecting either central government or construction firms alone.

The earlier summary of some of the costs and benefits accruing to an industrial estate development skated over a number of problematical points which are not present in the narrow investment appraisal approach. Some discussion of these points is necessary to get the feel of the difference between CBA and investment appraisal.

2. Objectives. CBA has the basic objective of identifying and valuing those costs and benefits which accrue to the investment, whether borne by the investing party itself or by any other party. The aim is to see if some policy objective, for example, easing congestion by building another Severn Bridge, can be achieved and also yield an overall net benefit. Another purpose is often to assist in making the best choice of alternative ways to achieve a single objective, as with the examination of four alternative sites for the third London Airport.

3. Cut-off points. When identifying costs and benefits, particularly those accruing to parties external to the investing party, it is difficult to know where to draw the boundary lines or cut-off points.

In the case of the industrial site development mentioned above, no reference was made to the possible loss of trade/income incurred by existing firms and their employees through lost custom. Such firms may currently be located many miles away or even at the other end of the country but may still be affected by this proposal.

In the case of a CBA on a new motorway, obvious costs and benefits are those accruing to users of the new road. However, if traffic is attracted from existing roads many miles away, should not the costs and benefits of residual users of those roads be considered?

Presumably the existing roads will be less congested and therefore vehicles run more economically and people will benefit from a saving in both work and leisure time. On the other hand traders providing services near to existing roads will suffer a loss of trade, just as service providers on the new road will gain trade and profit. The building of a new motorway will have a ripple effect like a stone in a pond. The costs and benefits will decrease in value as distance from the new road increases, but some effects could still be felt fifty miles away. Exactly where does the economist draw the line and stop looking for further costs or benefits?

There is no easy answer but a general approach would be to say when the costs and benefits cease to be significant in the context of that project.

4. Shadow prices. A problem arises when valuing social costs or benefits. Some commodities or services have no readily identifiable market price simply because they are not traded in the market place. 'Shadow price' is the name given to the imputed value for such transactions. It can be thought of as the opportunity cost of producing or consuming a commodity not generally bought and sold in the economy.

For example, in a CBA study of a new motorway, worktime saved by faster journeys could be valued at the normal rate of pay for the employees concerned. This is not the case with any leisure time saved. There is no rate of pay for leisure time so a shadow price or imputed value would have to be included for this particular benefit.

Even more difficult is the valuation of intangible costs such as noise or, for example, the loss of amenity through electrification of the railways and the consequent intrusion of pylons.

5. Discount rate. In a private sector investment appraisal the appropriate discount rate is the weighted average cost of capital of the firm concerned. For public sector investments the issue is not so simple and clear cut.

One reason is that the borrowing rate for a public body is not necessarily the free market rate, as it may be constrained by central government actions. Another reason is that members of the public may all place different values on the rate of interest needed to compensate them for saving as opposed to consuming goods and services now. However, one overall interest rate is needed.

(*a*) *Social opportunity cost of capital.* One solution is to take as the discount rate the rate of return on the projects foregone that allows the CBA project under review to go forward. This opportunity cost approach to the discount rate is known as the 'social opportunity cost of capital'. It is based on the logic that a public sector investment should do as well as any other public or private sector investment it displaces.

For example, assume that we find that the nominal DCF yield on marginal private sector investments is 13%. If a CBA on a public sector project finds a negative NPV when costs and benefits are discounted at this nominal rate of 13% then that project should be rejected.

(*b*) *Social time preference rate.* The alternative approach to finding a discount rate to use in CBA is for economists to derive the 'social time preference rate'. This represents the discount rate at which people equate future consumption with consumption now. One means used to calculate this discount rate is based on the hypothesis of 'diminishing marginal utility of consumption' but its calculation is outside the scope of this book.

As the social time preference rate and the social opportunity cost of capital do not necessarily lead to an identical figure, various compromise solutions have been suggested which combine these two rates into one composite discount rate.

6. Uncertainty. In any investment project there is bound to be uncertainty as to the value of the future stream of costs and benefits. This is true irrespective of whether the project undergoes a narrow investment appraisal or a wider view CBA.

The analysis of public sector projects by CBA can use the same risk analysis techniques as its private sector brethren. These include:

(*a*) setting a maximum payback period;
(*b*) sensitivity analysis to identify key variables or minimum required values;
(*c*) adding a risk premium to the discount rate varying with the degree of risk pertaining to each project;
(*d*) setting optimistic and pessimistic parameters in addition to the most likely values of yearly cash flows;
(*e*) use of subjective probability to quantify the likelihood of different values occurring for each variable;
(*f*) use of operational research techniques to find the expected DCF yield.

We saw above that there could be some difficulty in identifying a test discount rate to use in CBA. A useful sensitivity test that helps with this problem is to appraise public sector projects at various rates of discount. This determines whether a precise discount rate has significance for either acceptance of the project or the choice of the most attractive alternative design. If the decision is unaltered at both parameters of the range of discount rates then its precise calculation ceases to be a problem.

Summary

Capital projects of any kind should be appraised to see if they are worthwhile or to make the best choice from a number of alternatives. This is as true for projects in the public sector as it is for those in the private sector.

Certain public sector investments will be appraised, as in the private sector, when only the costs and benefits affecting the investing party are taken into account. The introduction of new technology into a local authority or decisions about replacement intervals for vehicle fleets are cases in point.

Other public sector investments, however, cannot usefully be appraised without taking into account the wider social costs and social benefits of every other affected party. This particularly applies to very large projects which often have considerable environmental effects. Cost–benefit analysis is the technique used to appraise these kinds of projects but very often pressure groups and political factors can be as influential as the financial recommendation.

Particular difficulties occur in CBAs that are not apparent in ordinary investment appraisals. These include the drawing of boundaries around a project when identifying the costs and benefits of affected parties. Valuing costs and benefits which have no readily identifiable market price is another distinguishing feature of CBA which uses shadow prices for this purpose. Finally, the choice of an appropriate discount rate to use in a CBA is another problematical area when resort is made to opportunity costs and time preference rates.

Progress test 11

1. Define 'cost-benefit analysis' as used for large public sector investments.
2. Identify the affected parties for a proposed underground rapid transport system in a provincial city.
3. Compare and contrast cost–benefit analysis with investment appraisal.
4. Explain how you would identify a shadow price for motor accidents in the context of a CBA on a new motorway system.
5. Contrast the calculation of an appropriate discount rate in the private sector with that appropriate to the public sector.

12

Conclusions

Previous chapters have outlined the techniques available to managers when making the important decision of whether, when and where to invest scarce capital. The superiority of discounting techniques over non-discounting techniques has been demonstrated by the need to take the time value of money into account.

Also vitally important is a consideration of taxation, inflation and risk and how these aspects impinge on the profitability of an investment. The prime advantage of the discounted cash flow appraisal method is that it is capable of manipulation to allow for these aspects. The benefits of using computers to perform these financial modelling tasks on significant project appraisals cannot be overstressed.

In the final analysis, though, it is people who take decisions not techniques. All the approaches discussed in this introductory book are only aids to decision-making. They help managers make better, or more rational decisions, but still allow them to use their initiative, or a feel for the market, by quantifying the likelihood of success.

Mathematical models of expected events do not necessarily give concrete answers. Their usefulness lies more in giving weight to a desired course of action, or giving an alternative view of a complex problem.

Post audits

Firms are likely to monitor actual capital expenditure against the amount authorised on a regular basis, as outlined in the section on capital budgeting in Chapter 1. This ensures that no dramatic overspends occur on any one project without further top management approval.

Firms should make known that it is company policy to carry out a post-audit on investment projects. This means that when the investment proceeds through its various stages of commissioning to operation, the actual cash flows should be compared with the expected events.

This checking will include capital and operating costs, sales price and volume, commissioning periods and other items. Special attention should be paid to any cash flow items that were found to be significant in sensitivity tests carried out at the initial appraisal stage. Once the project is fully operational a new estimate of the return earned can be compared with the predicted DCF yield.

To omit this post-audit activity means that valuable information is not fed back to the manager concerned to allow him to gain the experience necessary to improve his future forecasts. Human nature being what it is, the lack of a backward glance will inevitably lead to managers 'estimating' cash flows sufficient to justify acceptance of their pet projects.

There is a case to be made for allocating capital to people rather than allocating it to projects. One manager may have a good name for proposing investment initiatives which, on balance, prove to be as profitable as his estimates predicted. Surely he/she is a more worthy recipient of the firm's scarce investment funds as opposed to another manager who consistently over-estimates the profitability of his schemes?

Criticisms of the DCF yield method

It is hoped by this stage that the basic technique of DCF is not regarded as complicated, which is a criticism sometimes levied. Calculations of present value are easy to do with hand-held calculators, or with a microcomputer using a simple program like the one in Appendix 5. The real difficulty lies in preparing the estimated yearly cash flows but this applies to all methods of appraisal, including even the most rudimentary ones.

More tedious calculations are involved when taking account of inflation and other risks. These have been explained at some length to communicate the purpose and mechanics of such an exercise, not to suggest that an individual manager will perform all the calculations manually himself.

In the first place, sophisticated risk treatment is often reserved for projects using a significant amount of capital which eliminates many smaller projects. Secondly, it has been mentioned that computer manufacturers have standard programs which should fit a firm's requirements when evaluating risk, and which can be run by the company accountant if necessary.

The purpose of this book is to acquaint managers with techniques that allow them to consider all relevant aspects of an investment. This puts them on an equal footing with the financial specialist, but also helps them to identify new and profitable opportunities, without which firms stagnate.

In previous chapters we have seen that the NPV method and the DCF yield can give conflicting signals. This occurs in the two special situations of capital rationing and the choice between mutually exclusive investments. Provided we follow the relevant rule for each case this apparent conflict is no real problem.

1. Multiple yields. Another criticism sometimes levied at the DCF yield method is that it occasionally throws up more than one solution rate of interest for the same project. Which one then should we take as being correct? The problem only arises where there are negative net cash flows in a later year(s) after positive cash flows have already been achieved on the investment.

It is possible to have as many DCF yields as there are changes in sign in the cash flows. For example, a 'normal' investment has one change from negative cash outlay on the investment to positive cash flows earned on that investment in subsequent years.

In this case, provided the cash inflows exceed the cash outflows in total before discounting, there can only be one positive DCF yield as there is only one change of sign from negative to positive. However, if a replacement investment is required during the project life, which exceeds the cash inflow in the same year, there will be three changes of sign and possibly three DCF yields.

If we use the NPV method none of this is a problem, no matter how many changes of sign in the cash flows occur. When using the

DCF yield method, the easiest way around the problem is to discount any negative cash flow arising during, or at the end of, a project's life back to the previous year when it is covered by positive cash flows.

This discounting is done at the required rate of return for the company in question using the present value factor for Year 1 to bring it back to its previous year's equivalent value. The DCF yield is then calculated in the normal way, now being called the 'extended DCF yield'. It should be appreciated that the negative cash flows arising from tax payments in the last year are not usually significant in this context but can be discounted back to the previous year as described above.

Conflict with the profit and loss account

When firms invest in substantial projects taking two or three years to construct and commission, the effect on the profit and loss account is quite marked. Interest on any borrowed capital invested in the new project will appear as an expense, and thereby reduce profits, unless such interest is capitalised and added to the investment cost.

The alternative financing method of new share capital raised for the specific project means that pre-existing profits are apportioned over the now larger number of shares resulting in a worse performance. When the new project starts to yield profits this situation alters dramatically. Up to the commissioning stage however the profit and loss account will appear at variance with the DCF yield no matter how profitable the investment is expected to be over its whole life.

The directors of companies facing this situation may sometimes reject large projects on the grounds that it will adversely affect published profits for a year or two. In no way is this a criticism of the appraisal method but only a truism that the short-term view of one year does not necessarily equate with profitability measured over the project's whole life. This can be overcome by careful preparation of the shareholders to both the short- and long-term effects.

The nature of investment decisions inevitably means the prediction of future events and therefore luck may play a part in the actual outcome. Good investments depend on the generation of ideas, the use of suitable techniques and management control of the project at all stages. Good luck!

Further reading

Levy, H. and M. Sarnat, *Capital Investment and Financial Decision*, Prentice-Hall 1986.
Pike, R. and R. Dobbins, *Investment Decisions and Financial Strategy*, Philip Allan 1985.

Progress test 12

1. Why should a firm want to carry out post audits of substantial capital investment projects once they have been implemented?
2. 'DCF and NPV techniques are too complicated and can give conflicting signals. Why not stick to the old tried and trusted methods of payback period and accounting rate of return'? Discuss.
3. 'I am not going to authorise a project that lowers company profits next year no matter how profitable you say it will be'. (Managing Director). Discuss.

Appendices

Appendix 1
Case studies

Case study 1: A lease or buy appraisal illustrating aspects of taxation and the timing of lease payments

Carfax Limited have decided to computerise their stores issues to facilitate stocktaking and re-ordering. This decision was made after a thorough investigation into alternative systems and the likely benefits to be obtained. Management have gone firm on a particular supplier's equipment and related software. They now face the further decision whether to purchase outright or to take up the offer of leasing terms on a fixed price contract for the next five years.

If they buy outright, the total installation will cost £200,000 payable as soon as the system is working to their satisfaction. After one year's free maintenance, Carfax will take out a service contract to commence at the start of Year 2. The current cost of this maintenance is £2,000 payable at the beginning of each year, but it will increase in line with inflation estimated at 10 per cent per annum. There is not expected to be any residual value of the equipment at the end of its useful life of five years.

Alternatively, Carfax can lease the installation at an annual rent of £72,000, inclusive of maintenance, payable yearly in advance. These payments apply for the first five years, after which time the lease can be extended if the installation remains in use. The yearly payments for this later period reduce to 5 per cent of the initial cost of the installation.

Carfax require a minimum nominal return of 20 per cent after tax even though their nominal cost of capital is less. The reasoning applied by management is that if they purchase outright they will not be able to invest in other projects yielding a 20 per cent return or more. We can compare the two alternative methods of financing by calculating the NPV cost of each. Initially these calculations are performed using the normal year-end discounting convention as follows:

Net present value cost of the purchase alternative

Year	*Costs* £	*25% p.a capital allowances*	*35% tax saved* £	*Net cash flow* £	*PV factors at 20%*	*PV* £
0	−200,000			−200,000	1.000	−200,000
1	−2,200	50,000		− 2,200	.833	− 1,833
2	−2,420	37,500	+18,270	+ 15,850	.694	+ 11,000
3	−2,662	28,125	+13,972	+ 11,310	.579	+ 6,548
4	−2,928	21,094	+10,775	+ 7,847	.482	+ 3,782
5		63,281	+ 8,408	+ 8,408	.402	+ 3,380
6			+22,148	+ 22,148	.335	+ 7,420
					NPV	− £169,703

Net present value cost of the leasing alternative

Year	*Lease payments* £	*35% tax saved* £	*Net cash flow* £	*PV factors at 20%*	*PV* £
0	−72,000		− 72,000	1.000	− 72,000
1	−72,000	+25,200	− 46,800		
2	−72,000	+25,200	− 46,800	2.589	− 121,165
3	−72,000	+25,200	− 46,800		
4	−72,000	+25,200	− 46,800		
5		+25,200	+25,200	.402	+ 10,130
				NPV	− £183,035

On a strict interpretation of the NPVs of the alternatives it appears that buying is some £13,000 cheaper but this is subject to some comments on the calculations now mentioned:

1 The service contract is payable at the end of Year 1 in respect of Year 2 and the £2,200 represents the original £2,000 enhanced by 10 per cent inflation. Later years are similarly increased by 10 per cent p.a. with the last payment occurring at the end of Year 4 in respect of Year 5.

2 Payments for the service contract will be an allowable expense for tax purposes as they reduce otherwise taxable profits. Owing to the time lag in making corporation tax payments, the amount of tax saved will accordingly be lagged one year and is combined with tax saved on the capital allowances in the calculations above.

3 If the purchase takes place early in the accounting year the tax savings on the capital allowances will be lagged two years. This assumption has been made here so as not to make the purchase alternative look more attractive than may be the case. If only a one-year lag were to apply to the tax saved by capital allowances this reduces the NPV cost and makes purchasing even more attractive.

4 Lease payments are also an allowable expense against tax so these tax savings are subject to the same time lag as in note 2.

5 If the useful life of the installation does not reach five years Carfax is tied to the financial agreements expressed in the NPV calculations above and the choice is not affected. If the life exceeds five years the service payments will continue on the purchase alternative or the leasing payments reduce to £10,000 p.a. less tax relief. Such longer life makes leasing even less attractive although the PV factors are relatively small at Year 6 and beyond.

6 It has been assumed in the interest calculations that all financial transactions occur at yearly intervals. This is probably valid for all cash flows bar the lease payments of £72,000 p.a. If these payments occur throughout the year, rather than in full at the start of each year, their present value cost will be reduced in Years 0-4 as money is paid out later than it would be at the start of each year.
The following figures summarise the difference:

PV cost of 5 yearly payments of £72,000 at the start of each year	£258,408
PV cost of 5 total payments of £72,000 p.a. spread over each year	£227,520
Difference	£ 30,888

This latter assumption is crucial as it reverses the previous choice of the purchasing alternative as the more attractive.

Case study 2: Example of a replacement decision where alternative courses of action have different lives

The Seaton Engineering Co. are considering whether to replace or repair a particular machine which has just broken down. Last year this machine cost £20,000 to run and maintain. These costs have been increasing in real terms in recent years with the age of the machine. A further useful life of five years is expected if immediate repairs costing £19,000 are carried out. If the machine is not repaired it will be sold immediately to realise about £5,000.

Alternatively, the company can buy a new machine for £49,000 with an expected life of ten years. In this case running and maintenance costs will reduce to £14,000 each year and are not expected to increase much in real terms for a few years at least. Seaton Engineering regard a nominal return of 20 per cent as a minimum requirement on any new investment.

A difficulty which arises in this situation is the difference in life expectancy between the two alternatives. Clearly we cannot use the total NPV cost over five years to compare with a NPV cost over ten years. If we assume replacement will take place after five years if we repair the existing machine, then we are faced with a fifteen year total which again is not comparable with ten years.

One way to tackle this problem of unequal lives is to compare alternatives on an annual cost basis. This technique was first mentioned in Chapter 10 and basically consists of reducing the capital cost to an annual basis. We do this by calculating what is equivalent to the yearly repayment on a building society mortgage.

The amount needed each year to repay £1 is the reciprocal of the cumulative present value factor for that year. For example, if we refer back to the end of Chapter 2, the annual repayment for each of six years on a £200,000 mortgage at 13 per cent is found from the calculation $\frac{£200,000}{3.998}$ = £50,025 or £50,000 in round terms.

We can now apply this technique to the replacement decision facing Seaton Engineering by comparing both alternatives on an annual cost basis which will take into account the different life expectancies.

Repair existing machine

	£
Resale value if sold now	5,000
Cost of repairs now	19,000
Total cost at Year 0	24,000
Annual equivalent cost (for five years)	8,024*
Running and maintenance cost p.a.	20,000
Total annual cost	£28,024

Buy replacement machine

Purchase cost of new machine at Year 0	49,000
Annual equivalent cost (for ten years)	11,689**
Running and maintenance costs p.a.	14,000
Total annual cost	£25,689
Difference in annual costs-in-use therefore	£2,335

*The annual equivalent cost has been calculated from $\frac{£24,000}{2.991}$

**The annual equivalent cost has been calculated from $\frac{£49,000}{4.192}$

(An alternative treatment of the £5,000 resale value of the existing machine is to omit it from the first calculation and deduct £5,000 from the cost of the new machine to give a net purchase cost of £44,000 in the second situation.)

The difference of £2,335 in the annual costs represents the saving achieved from buying the new replacement machine rather than repairing the old. This difference will widen if the real cost of operating the old machine increases with age, whilst the operating cost of the new machine does not change much for the next few years. Inflation will also widen the gap between the two alternatives having more effect on the higher running costs on the existing machine, so making the new machine even more attractive. Tax has been ignored for simplicity but would be allowed for in practice. Tax relief will apply to all the costs in both alternatives. A capital allowance of 25 per cent p.a. on a reducing balance basis will be claimed on the new machine, whereas repair and running costs will automatically get tax relief through their inclusion in the profit and loss account.

Case study 3: Illustration of an expansion/diversification project incorporating aspects of taxation and inflation

Progressive Ltd require a nominal return of 20 per cent after tax on any new investment. Management are considering a proposal to make and sell a new product by installing new plant in existing premises. No alternative use is envisaged for this space in the foreseeable future.

The initial investment totals £180,000 comprising £100,000 of new plant and £80,000 of working capital. A product life of five years is anticipated after which time the plant will have remaining value of about £10,000 at today's prices, and the working capital will be recovered. Situated in a Special Development Area, Progressive Ltd fully expect to receive a grant of 22 per cent of the cost of the new plant in about one year's time.

Sales are budgeted at £200,000 for each of the next five years and operating costs (excluding depreciation) are put at £150,000. Inflation will affect both of these figures which are expressed at today's prices. The rate of inflation is expected to be about 10 per cent p.a. and will also affect working capital requirements and the resale value of the plant. This estimate of inflation is not regarded as too critical as increased costs can be quickly recovered with little effect on sales volume.

Corporation tax is currently 35 per cent and a 25 per cent p.a. capital allowance based on the reducing balance is available. A two-year lag is assumed by Progressive Ltd for such savings.

The various constituent items of the net cash flow can be set out in separate columns for simplicity and a present value calculation conducted at the minimum required rate of 20 per cent as shown below.

Calculation of the NPV at 20% on an expansion project assuming 10% inflation applies to all relevant cash flows

Year	*Plant*	*Capital allowances*	*35% tax saved on CAs*	*Working capital*	*Taxable profit*	*35% tax on profit*
	£		£	£	£	£
0	–100,000			– 80,000		
1	+ 22,000	25,000		– 8,000	+55,000	
2	(grant)	18,750	+8,750	– 8,800	+60,500	–19,250
3		14,062	+6,562	– 9,680	+66,550	–21,175
4		10,547	+4,922	– 10,648	+73,205	–23,292
5	+ 16,105	15,536	+3,691	+117,128	+80,525	–25,622
6	(resale)		+5,438			–28,184

Year	*Net cash flows*	*20% PV factors*	*PV*	*30% PV factors*	*PV*
	£		£		£
0	– 180,000	1.000	–180,000	1.000	–180,000
1	+ 69,000	.833	+ 57,477	.769	+ 53,061
2	+ 41,200	.694	+ 28,593	.592	+ 24,390
3	+ 42,257	.579	+ 24,467	.455	+ 19,227
4	+ 44,187	.482	+ 21,298	.350	+ 15,465
5	+191,827	.402	+ 77,114	.269	+ 51,601
6	– 22,746	.335	– 7,620	.207	– 4,708
		NPV	+£ 21,329	NPV	–£ 20,964

The surplus NPV of £21,329 when discounted at 20 per cent indicates that a considerably higher rate of interest could have been deducted. Progressive can discover this solution rate (i.e. DCF yield) by trial and error. Supposing the 30 per cent rate of interest was chosen as illustrated, the NPV now becomes a deficit of £20,964.

By interpolation of the two NPVs at 20 per cent and 30 per cent it appears that every 1 per cent change in the discount rate alters the NPV by about £4,200. To eliminate the NPV surplus of £21,329 will require an increase in the 20 per cent interest rate of about 5 per cent. The DCF yield can therefore be interpolated at about 25 per cent which we would go on to calculate in practice.

After allowing for inflation at 10 per cent on the relevant cash flows and incorporating all tax transactions in the year that they occur we can assume Progressive's management will accept this project as quite viable. The expected DCF yield of 25 per cent comfortably exceeds the 20 per cent minimum required.

Further tests on the sensitivity of the return to variations in the cash flows can be carried out or probabilities applied to different sets of cash flows. These matters are discussed in previous chapters and applied in a later case study.

Case study 4: Illustration of the use of probability theory in dealing with uncertain future costs and revenues

The management of Shop Developers Limited are considering the feasibility of a new development to build and let shops on the outskirts of a large town. Depending on the exact design of the buildings the capital cost will be between £2m and £2.2m with greater emphasis on the lower figure. More doubt exists as to the level of net rental income. It could be as low as £200,000 but with an attractive layout and a little luck it could be as much as £260,000 each year. The realistic life of the development is put at 25 years.

Shop Developers require a return on investment of 9 per cent. This may seem low but it should be borne in mind that much of the capital is borrowed at a fixed rate of interest which does not increase when rents are periodically reviewed. Such future increases in rent will compensate for inflation as well as reflect the demand for such properties.

To facilitate the decision whether to proceed with the development or not, the project team have been asked to assess the likelihood of the eventual outcomes. More specifically, they have been asked to assign probability factors to both the capital cost and the net income from rent. More than one value can be assumed for each of these variable items to cover the range of possibilities. The values chosen by the project team with their respective probability factors are shown below:

Capital cost	*Probability*	*Annual rent*	*Probability*
£2.0m	0.7	£200,000	0.1
£2.2m	0.3	£220,000	0.3
	1.0	£240,000	0.4
		£260,000	0.2
			1.0

Instead of calculating the DCF yield from just one estimate of rent and one capital cost it is possible to combine the likelihood of all the possible values in the computation. For example the weighted average capital cost can be expressed as:

£2.0m x 0.7	= £1.40m
£2.2m x 0.3	= £0.66m
Weighted average cost	= £2.06m

Similarly the four possible rent values can be used together with their respective probabilities to find the weighted average annual rent:

£200,000 x 0.1	= £ 20,000
£220,000 x 0.3	= £ 66,000
£240,000 x 0.4	= £ 96,000
£260,000 x 0.2	= £ 52,000
Weighted average rent	= £ 234,000 p.a.

The expected DCF yield can now be interpolated from the cumulative PV table for 25 years. The relevant factor is found from the calculation in £2.06m/£234,000 = 8.8 which equates to the 10 per cent rate of interest. The initial return on the investment is therefore expected to be 10 per cent which is the weighted average of all the possibilities considered.

The next question posed by the management of Shop Developers concerns the level of confidence that the project team have in the development yielding a satisfactory return of 9 per cent or more. There are eight possible combined events from the pairing of one of two capital costs with one of four annual rents. For each of these combined events we need to calculate the DCF yield and the probability of the two values combining together. The DCF yields are calculated from the cumulative PV table and the combined probability from the multiplication of the two relevant probabilities as shown below.

There is only one combined event which does not yield a satisfactory return. This occurs when the lowest rent envisaged combines with the highest capital cost to give a DCF yield of 8 per cent. The chance of this combination occurring is .03 or 3 per cent, whilst the chance of the rate of return being 9 per cent or more is 97 per cent. We can use this 97 per cent as the level of confidence Shop Developers have in a satisfactory outcome to the development. Because the expected DCF yield of 10 per cent is slightly higher than the minimum required and the level of confidence in a satisfactory outcome exceptionally high at 97 per cent we can assume this project will proceed.

	Capital cost			
	£2.0m (0.7)		*£2.2m (0.3)*	
Annual rent	*DCF yield*	*Combined probability*	*DCF yield*	*Combined probability*
£200,000 (.1)	9%	(.07)	8%	(.03)
£220,000 (.3)	10%	(.21)	9%	(.09)
£240,000 (.4)	11%	(.28)	10%	(.12)
£260,000 (.2)	12%	(.14)	11%	(.06)

Case study 5: Illustration of inflation being incorporated in the cash flows and its effect on a large terminal value

Gosforth Brewery Limited are considering refurbishing one of their managed houses at a cost of £50,000. The property is currently worth £200,000 and the refurbishing is expected to last five years by which time it is assumed the property will be worth £450,000.

The increase in trade resulting from refurbishing is valued at £12,000 for the first year and is expected to rise in line with inflation over the next four years at 10 per cent p.a.

The directors normally require a nominal return of a least 15 per cent and the appraisal below was put forward for their approval.

Just as they were about to approve this project on the grounds that is seemed to satisfy the minimum target rate of return of 15 per cent, one director queried this analysis. 'If the property is going to rise in value whether we refurbish or not,' he said, 'should we not justify the £50,000 investment in refurbishing by the increased profits from trade alone, excluding the rise in property value?'

		Net cash flow £	PV factors at 15%	PV £
Year	0	– 200,000 – 50,000	1.000	– 250,000
	1	+ 12,000	.870	+ 10,440
	2	+ 13,200	.756	+ 9,979
	3	+ 14,520	.658	+ 9,554
	4	+ 15,972	.572	+ 9,136
	5	+ 17,569 + 450,000	.497	+ 232,382
			NPV	+£ 21,491

(Note: Taxation is ignored in this example for clarity.)

After some heated discussion it was agreed to look at the project again and the accountant was requested to do some quick sums.

His revised appraisal now appeared to show that the increased trade did not justify the refurbishing cost:

		Net cash flow £	*PV factors at 15%*	*PV* £
Year	0	– 50,000	1.000	– 50,000
	1	+12,000	.870	+10,440
	2	+13,200	.756	+ 9,979
	3	+14,520	.658	+ 9,554
	4	+15,972	.572	+ 9,136
	5	+17,569	.497	+ 8,732
			NPV	–£ 2,159

The directors were unwilling to approve the scheme and asked the marketing director to consider ways of increasing trade to make the scheme viable. The amount of extra trade required can be calculated by a further trial and interpolation of the results. Assuming £13,000 was chosen as the first year value the NPV calculation results in a surplus as follows:

		Net cash flow £	*PV factors at 15%*	*PV* £
Year	0	– 50,000	1.000	– 50,000
	1	+13,000	.870	+ 11,310
	2	+14,300	.756	+ 10,811
	3	+15,730	.658	+ 10,350
	4	+17,303	.572	+ 9,897
	5	+19,033	.497	+ 9,459
			NPV	+£ 1,827

By interpolation the increase in initial trade required to give a 15 per cent return on the refurbishing cost is about £12,500 as the NPVs of –£2,159 and +£1,827 are almost equidistant to the zero NPV required for a 15 per cent return.

Case study 6: Illustration of life-cycle costing applied to a physical asset already in use

Durham Brewery have a steady market for one of their bottled beers and have recently installed a new bottle-washing and -filling machine of a different type to that previously used. The project team were keen to know how the machine performed against the manufacturer's specification and their own estimates. With this in mind they prepared a life cycle cost budget for the new machine and decided to monitor the actual costs-in-use. A summary of the LCC budget is shown below together with the actual costs for the first year of operation.

In general terms the machine performed very much as expected except in one important area. A certain amount of bottle breakage and associated beer losses are inevitable and a reasonable allowance was made by the project team in the light of experience. The actual cost of the breakages and spoilt beer was nearly twice the amount predicted in the budget. Compared to the capital cost for the year these bottling losses were twice the cost of the machine itself. It was apparent that substantial savings would result from the elimination of the source of the malfunction. Engineering studies were carried out and modifications to the machine were implemented. The manufacturer was also involved even though the brewery carried out their own modification. Without feedback from such users, manufacturers are not able to 'design-out' faults and imperfections. Only £20,000 was spent on the modification and this was repaid by the savings achieved in the first year.

Life cycle cost of bottle-washing and -filling machine

	Annual costs			
	Budget £	%	*Actual* £	
Capital	22,000	16.6	22,000	Annual equivalent cost of purchase and installation
Operation	9,800	7.4	10,150	Labour
	39,000	29.5	37,820	Steam
	15,000	11.3	15,700	Electricity
	9,000	6.8	8,750	Water
Maintenance	8,700	6.6	12,500	Labour
	3,200	2.4	7,590	Materials and parts
	500	0.4	500	Holding costs of parts
Bottling losses	25,000	18.9	47,350	Glass breakage and beer spillage
	£132,200	100%	£162,360	

(Note: The total beer cost is not included as a cost of the machine.)

Case study 7: Illustration of life-cycle cost data used to formulate a replacement policy

Buzby National Telephone Service use a substantial fleet of vans of varying ages up to four years old. Each van has an individual asset number against which all fuel, oil, maintenance and repair costs are charged. Using this data it has been possible to extract the trends of the costs relative to the age of the vehicle. These costs were then converted to today's prices by use of appropriate price indices. The following information relating to the present type of vehicle is all expressed in current purchasing power £s:

1 Purchase cost of new van £6,000
2 Trade-in value when: One year old £4,000
Two years old £2,500
Three years old £1,300
Four years old £500
3 Fuel consumption increases with the age of the vehicle partly through wear but also because the design improvements of more recent models result in fuel economies. Maintenance, repair and parts replacement also increase in cost as the vehicle ages, particularly after two years. These costs (at today's prices) are as follows:

	Fuel cost p.a.	*Maintenance and repair cost p.a.*
0-1 Years	£2,500	£200
1-2 Years	£2,600	£350
2-3 Years	£2,820	£700
3-4 Years	£3,200	£1,750

The nominal cost of borrowing from the government is about 15.5 per cent. A nominal rate is used to discount cash flows expressed in future value £s. The above costs are all expressed at today's prices and are not inflated year by year for inflation expected to fluctuate around 10 per cent p.a. There are therefore two alternative procedures we can follow. We can either inflate all costs and values by 10 per cent p.a. and discount the LCC at 15.5 per cent, or we can leave the money values in today's £s and discount the LCC at 5 per cent. (With inflation at 10 per cent p.a. a nominal return of 15.5 per cent equates to a real return of 5 per cent.) For simplicity of explanation of the yearly cash flows the latter course of action is adopted here and a 5 per cent discount rate is used in the present value calculation.

If vehicles can be kept up to four years it is essential to examine the possibility of replacing them up to this age. Therefore Buzby is faced with four alternative replacement intervals – when the vans are one year, two years, three years and four years old respectively. The lowest common multiple of these four replacement intervals is twelve years for which period we shall compute the net present value of the life cycle costs as follows:

LCC of a service van assuming replacement each year for a total period of twelve years

(1) Year	(2) Purchase cost	(3) Trade-in value	(4) Fuel cost	(5) Maintenance and repair cost	(6) Net cash flow	(7) PV factors at 5%	(8) PV
	£	£	£	£	£		£
0	-6,000				- 6,000	1.000	- 6,000
1	-6,000	+4,000	-2,500	-200	-4,700		
2	-6,000	+4,000	-2,500	-200	- 4,700		
3	-6,000	+4,000	-2,500	-200	- 4,700		
4	-6,000	+4,000	-2,500	-200	- 4,700		
5	-6,000	+4,000	-2,500	-200	- 4,700		
6	-6,000	+4,000	-2,500	-200	- 4,700	8.306	-39,038
7	-6,000	+4,000	-2,500	-200	- 4,700		
8	-6,000	+4,000	-2,500	-200	- 4,700		
9	-6,000	+4,000	-2,500	-200	- 4,700		
10	-6,000	+4,000	-2,500	-200	- 4,700		
11	-6,000	+4,000	-2,500	-200	- 4,700		
12	-	+4,000	-2,500	-200	+1,300	.557	+ 724
						NPV	- £44,314

The cost of buying and running one service van and replacing it at the end of each year has a total PV cost of £44,314 over a twelve year period. This can now be compared with the equivalent PV cost on the assumption that the van is replaced every two years instead of each year as follows in the analysis opposite:

The cost of buying and running a service van and replacing it every two years can be seen to be less than the NPV cost of £44,314 resulting from replacing each year. We now need to calculate similar NPVs for a three year replacement interval and a four year interval. The reader can attempt these for himself and will find them to be £42,752 and £44,874 respectively. We can summarise the results as follows.

Replacement interval	*NPV cost*
One year	£44,314
Two years	£42,810
Three years	£42,752
Four years	£44,874

LCC of a service van assuming replacement every two years for a total period of twelve years

(1) Year	(2) Purchase cost £	(3) Trade-in value £	(4) Fuel cost £	(5) Maintenance and repair cost £	(6) Net cash flow £	(7) PV factors at 5%	(8) PV £
0	- 6,000				- 6,000	1.000	- 6,000
1			- 2,500	- 200	- 2,700	.952	- 2,570
2	- 6,000	+2,500	- 2,600	- 350	- 6,450	.907	- 5,850
3			- 2,500	- 200	- 2,700	.864	- 2,333
4	- 6,000	+2,500	- 2,600	- 350	- 6,450	.823	- 5,308
5			- 2,500	- 200	- 2,700	.784	- 2,117
6	- 6,000	+2,500	- 2,600	- 350	- 6,450	.746	- 4,812
7			- 2,500	- 200	- 2,700	.711	- 1,920
8	- 6,000	+2,500	- 2,600	- 350	- 6,450	.677	- 4,367
9			- 2,500	- 200	- 2,700	.645	- 1,742
10	- 6,000	+2,500	- 2,600	- 350	- 6,450	.614	- 3,960
11			- 2,500	- 200	- 2,700	.585	- 1,580
12		+2,500	- 2,600	- 350	- 450	.557	- 251
						NPV	- £ 42,810

From inspection it can be seen that the one year and four year replacement intervals are not the cheapest but that replacing every two or three years would be more economic. There is little to choose between the costs of the middle values and the replacement policy will be determined by non-financial factors like image.

NOTE: The alternative approach of inflating the yearly cash flows and discounting at the nominal rate of 15.5 per cent will lead to exactly the same result and will have to be adopted when we cannot make the assumption that all costs and trade-in values will inflate at an equal rate. In the private sector we must also incorporate tax transactions in the yearly cash flows.

Appendix 2

Present value of £1

Year	5%	6%	7%	8%	9%	10%	11%	12%	13%	14%	15%	16%	17%	18%
0	1.000	1.000	1.000	1.000	1.000	1.000	1.000	1.000	1.000	1.000	1.000	1.000	1.000	1.000
1	.952	.943	.935	.926	.917	.909	.901	.893	.885	.877	.870	.862	.855	.847
2	.907	.890	.873	.857	.842	.826	.812	.797	.783	.769	.756	.743	.731	.718
3	.864	.840	.816	.794	.772	.751	.731	.712	.693	.675	.658	.641	.624	.609
4	.823	.792	.763	.735	.708	.683	.659	.636	.613	.592	.572	.552	.534	.516
5	.784	.747	.713	.681	.650	.621	.593	.567	.543	.519	.497	.476	.456	.437
6	.746	.705	.666	.630	.596	.564	.535	.507	.480	.456	.432	.410	.390	.370
7	.711	.665	.623	.583	.547	.513	.482	.452	.425	.400	.376	.354	.333	.314
8	.677	.627	.582	.540	.502	.467	.434	.404	.376	.351	.327	.305	.285	.266
9	.645	.592	.544	.500	.460	.424	.391	.361	.333	.308	.284	.263	.243	.225
10	.614	.558	.508	.463	.422	.386	.352	.322	.295	.270	.247	.227	.208	.191
11	.585	.527	.475	.429	.388	.350	.317	.287	.261	.237	.215	.195	.178	.162
12	.557	.497	.444	.397	.356	.319	.286	.257	.231	.208	.187	.168	.152	.137
13	.530	.469	.415	.368	.326	.290	.258	.229	.204	.182	.163	.145	.130	.116
14	.505	.442	.388	.340	.299	.263	.232	.205	.181	.160	.141	.125	.111	.099
15	.481	.417	.362	.315	.275	.239	.209	.183	.160	.140	.123	.108	.095	.084
16	.458	.394	.339	.292	.252	.218	.188	.163	.141	.123	.107	.093	.081	.071
17	.436	.371	.317	.270	.231	.198	.170	.148	.125	.108	.093	.080	.069	.060
18	.416	.350	.296	.250	.212	.180	.153	.130	.111	.095	.081	.069	.059	.051
19	.396	.331	.277	.232	.194	.164	.138	.116	.098	.083	.070	.060	.051	.043
20	.377	.312	.258	.215	.178	.149	.124	.104	.087	.073	.061	.051	.043	.037
25	.295	.233	.184	.146	.116	.092	.074	.059	.047	.038	.030	.025	.020	.016
30	.231	.174	.131	.099	.075	.057	.044	.033	.026	.020	.015	.012	.009	.007
35	.181	.130	.094	.068	.049	.036	.026	.019	.014	.010	.008	.006	.004	.003
40	.142	.097	.067	.046	.032	.022	.015	.011	.008	.005	.004	.003	.002	.001
45	.111	.073	.048	.031	.021	.014	.009	.006	.004	.003	.002	.001	.001	.001
50	.087	.054	.034	.021	.013	.009	.005	.003	.002	.001	.001	.001	.000	.000

Note: The above present value factors are based on year-end interest calculations

19%	20%	21%	22%	23%	24%	25%	26%	27%	28%	29%	30%	35%	40%
1.000	1.000	1.000	1.000	1.000	1.000	1.000	1.000	1.000	1.000	1.000	1.000	1.000	1.000
.840	.833	.826	.820	.813	.807	.800	.794	.787	.781	.775	.769	.741	.714
.706	.694	.683	.672	.661	.650	.640	.630	.620	.610	.601	.592	.549	.510
.593	.579	.564	.551	.537	.524	.512	.500	.488	.477	.466	.455	.406	.364
.499	.482	.467	.451	.437	.423	.410	.397	.384	.373	.361	.350	.301	.260
.419	.402	.386	.370	.355	.341	.328	.315	.303	.291	.280	.269	.223	.186
.352	.335	.319	.303	.289	.275	.262	.250	.238	.227	.217	.207	.165	.133
.296	.279	.263	.249	.235	.222	.210	.198	.188	.178	.168	.159	.122	.095
.249	.233	.218	.204	.191	.179	.168	.157	.148	.139	.130	.123	.091	.068
.209	.194	.180	.167	.155	.144	.134	.125	.116	.108	.101	.094	.067	.048
.176	.162	.149	.137	.126	.116	.107	.099	.092	.085	.078	.073	.050	.035
.148	.135	.123	.112	.103	.094	.086	.079	.072	.066	.061	.056	.037	.025
.124	.112	.102	.092	.083	.076	.069	.062	.057	.052	.047	.043	.027	.018
.104	.093	.084	.075	.068	.061	.055	.050	.045	.040	.037	.033	.020	.013
.088	.078	.069	.062	.055	.049	.044	.039	.035	.032	.028	.025	.015	.009
.074	.065	.057	.051	.045	.040	.035	.031	.028	.025	.022	.020	.011	.006
.062	.054	.047	.042	.036	.032	.028	.025	.022	.019	.017	.015	.008	.005
.052	.045	.039	.034	.030	.026	.023	.020	.017	.015	.013	.012	.006	.003
.044	.038	.032	.028	.024	.021	.018	.016	.014	.012	.010	.009	.005	.002
.037	.031	.027	.023	.020	.017	.014	.012	.011	.009	.008	.007	.003	.002
.031	.026	.022	.019	.016	.014	.012	.010	.008	.007	.006	.005	.002	.001
.013	.011	.009	.007	.006	.005	.004	.003	.003	.002	.002	.001	.001	.000
.005	.004	.003	.003	.002	.002	.001	.001	.001	.001	.000	.000	.000	.000
.002	.002	.001	.001	.001	.001	.000	.000	.000	.000	.000	.000	.000	.000
.001	.001	.000	.000	.000	.000	.000	.000	.000	.000	.000	.000	.000	.000
.000	.000	.000	.000	.000	.000	.000	.000	.000	.000	.000	.000	.000	.000
.000	.000	.000	.000	.000	.000	.000	.000	.000	.000	.000	.000	.000	.000

Appendix 3

Cumulative present value of £1 per annum

Year	5%	6%	7%	8%	9%	10%	11%	12%	13%
1	.952	.943	.935	.926	.917	.909	.901	.893	.885
2	1.859	1.833	1.808	1.783	1.759	1.736	1.713	1.690	1.668
3	2.723	2.673	2.624	2.577	2.531	2.487	2.444	2.402	2.361
4	3.546	3.465	3.387	3.312	3.240	3.170	3.102	3.037	2.974
5	4.329	4.212	4.100	3.993	3.890	3.791	3.696	3.605	3.517
6	5.076	4.917	4.767	4.623	4.486	4.355	4.231	4.111	3.998
7	5.786	5.582	5.389	5.206	5.033	4.868	4.712	4.564	4.423
8	6.463	6.210	5.971	5.747	5.535	5.335	5.146	4.968	4.799
9	7.108	6.802	6.515	6.247	5.995	5.759	5.537	5.328	5.132
10	7.722	7.360	7.024	6.710	6.418	6.145	5.889	5.650	5.426
11	8.306	7.887	7.499	7.139	6.805	6.495	6.207	5.938	5.687
12	8.863	8.384	7.943	7.536	7.161	6.814	6.492	6.194	5.918
13	9.394	8.853	8.358	7.904	7.487	7.103	6.750	6.424	6.122
14	9.899	9.295	8.745	8.244	7.786	7.367	6.982	6.628	6.302
15	10.380	9.712	9.108	8.559	8.061	7.606	7.191	6.811	6.462
16	10.838	10.106	9.447	8.851	8.313	7.824	7.379	6.974	6.604
17	11.274	10.477	9.763	9.122	8.544	8.022	7.549	7.120	6.729
18	11.690	10.828	10.059	9.372	8.756	8.201	7.702	7.250	6.840
19	12.085	11.158	10.336	9.604	8.950	8.365	7.839	7.366	6.938
20	12.462	11.470	10.594	9.818	9.129	8.514	7.963	7.469	7.025
25	14.094	12.783	11.654	10.675	9.823	9.077	8.422	7.843	7.330
30	15.372	13.765	12.409	11.258	10.274	9.427	8.694	8.055	7.496
35	16.374	14.498	12.948	11.655	10.567	9.644	8.855	8.176	7.586
40	17.159	15.046	13.332	11.925	10.757	9.779	8.951	8.244	7.634
45	17.774	15.456	13.606	12.108	10.881	9.863	9.008	8.283	7.661
50	18.256	15.762	13.801	12.234	10.962	9.915	9.042	8.305	7.675

Note: The above present value factors are based on year-end interest calculations

14%	15%	16%	17%	18%	19%	20%	21%	22%	23%
.877	.870	.862	.855	.847	.840	.833	.826	.820	.813
1.647	1.626	1.605	1.585	1.566	1.546	1.528	1.510	1.492	1.474
2.322	2.200	2.240	2.210	2.174	2.140	2.106	2.074	2.042	2.011
2.914	2.855	2.798	2.743	2.690	2.639	2.589	2.540	2.494	2.448
3.433	3.352	3.274	3.199	3.127	3.058	2.991	2.926	2.864	2.804
3.889	3.784	3.685	3.589	3.498	3.410	3.326	3.245	3.167	3.092
4.288	4.160	4.039	3.922	3.812	3.706	3.605	3.508	3.416	3.327
4.639	4.487	4.344	4.207	4.078	3.954	3.837	3.726	3.619	3.518
4.946	4.772	4.607	4.451	4.303	4.163	4.031	3.905	3.786	3.673
5.216	5.019	4.833	4.659	4.494	4.339	4.192	4.054	3.923	3.799
5.453	5.234	5.029	4.836	4.656	4.486	4.327	4.177	4.035	3.902
5.660	5.421	5.197	4.988	4.793	4.610	4.439	4.278	4.127	3.985
5.842	5.583	5.342	5.118	4.910	4.715	4.533	4.362	4.203	4.053
6.002	5.724	5.468	5.229	5.008	4.802	4.611	4.432	4.265	4.108
6.142	5.847	5.575	5.324	5.092	4.876	4.675	4.490	4.315	4.153
6.265	5.954	5.669	5.405	5.162	4.938	4.730	4.536	4.357	4.190
6.373	6.047	5.749	5.475	5.222	4.990	4.775	4.576	4.391	4.219
6.467	6.128	5.818	5.534	5.273	5.033	4.812	4.608	4.419	4.243
6.550	6.198	5.877	5.584	5.316	5.070	4.844	4.635	4.442	4.263
6.623	6.259	5.929	5.628	5.353	5.101	4.870	4.657	4.460	4.279
6.873	6.464	6.097	5.766	5.467	5.195	4.948	4.721	4.514	4.323
7.003	6.566	6.177	5.829	5.517	5.235	4.979	4.746	4.534	4.339
7.070	6.617	6.215	5.858	5.539	5.251	4.992	4.756	4.541	4.345
7.105	6.642	6.234	5.871	5.548	5.258	4.997	4.760	4.544	4.347
7.123	6.654	6.242	5.877	5.552	5.261	4.999	4.761	4.545	4.347
7.133	6.661	6.246	5.880	5.554	5.262	5.000	4.762	4.545	4.348

Year	24%	25%	26%	27%	28%	29%	30%	35%	40%
1	.807	.800	.794	.787	.781	.775	.769	.741	.714
2	1.457	1.440	1.424	1.407	1.392	1.376	1.361	1.289	1.224
3	1.981	1.952	1.923	1.896	1.868	1.842	1.816	1.696	1.589
4	2.404	2.362	2.320	2.280	2.241	2.203	2.166	1.997	1.849
5	2.745	2.689	2.635	2.583	2.532	2.483	2.436	2.220	2.035
6	3.021	2.951	2.885	2.821	2.759	2.700	2.643	2.385	2.168
7	3.242	3.161	3.083	3.009	2.937	2.868	2.802	2.508	2.263
8	3.421	3.329	3.241	3.156	3.076	2.999	2.925	2.598	2.331
9	3.566	3.463	3,366	3.273	3.184	3.100	3.019	2.665	2.379
10	3.682	3.571	3.465	3.366	3.269	3.178	3.092	2.715	2.414
11	3.776	3.656	3.544	3.437	3.335	3.239	3.147	2.752	2.438
12	3.851	3.725	3.606	3.493	3.387	3.286	3.190	2.779	2.456
13	3.912	3.780	3.656	3.538	3.427	3.322	3.223	2.799	2.469
14	3.962	3.824	3.695	3.573	3.459	3.351	3.249	2.814	2.478
15	4.001	3.859	3.726	3.601	3.483	3.373	3.268	2.825	2.484
16	4.033	3.887	3.751	3.623	3.503	3.390	3.283	2.834	2.489
17	4.059	3.910	3.771	3.640	3.518	3.403	3.295	2.840	2.492
18	4.080	3.928	3.786	3.654	3.529	3.413	3.304	2.844	2.494
19	4.097	3.942	3.799	3.666	3.539	3.421	3.311	2.848	2.496
20	4.110	3.954	3.808	3.673	3.546	3.427	3.316	2.850	2.497
25	4.147	3.985	3.834	3.694	3.564	3.442	3.329	2.856	2.499
30	4.160	3.995	3.842	3.701	3.569	3.447	3.332	2.857	2.500
35	4.164	3.998	3.845	3.703	3.571	3.448	3.333	2.857	2.500
40	4.166	3.999	3.846	3.703	3.571	3.448	3.333	2.857	2.500
45	4.166	4.000	3.846	3.704	3.571	3.448	3.333	2.857	2.500
50	4.167	4.000	3.846	3.704	3.571	3.448	3.333	2.857	2.500

Appendix 4
Glossary of terms

advance corporation tax
A part of the total corporation tax liability which is paid to the Inland Revenue at the time a dividend is paid to shareholders.

balance sheet
A statement of the financial position of a firm at a point in time showing the assets owned and the sources of finance.

beta factor
A measurement of risk used in setting the appropriate discounting rate in an appraisal.

capital allowance
The Inland Revenue's equivalent of a company's depreciation charge. Allowances are granted on purchases of certain new assets and they reduce taxable profits.

capital asset pricing model (CAPM)
A method of setting the appropriate discount rate in an appraisal.

capital expenditure
Expenditure on fixed assets with a life expectancy of more than one accounting period.

capital gearing
See gearing.

corporation tax
The tax levied on a limited company's profit. There is one basic rate (currently 35 per cent) but a small company rate (of 25 per cent) applies to companies earning low profits.

cost benefit analysis
A wider investment appraisal technique mainly used on large public sector projects incorporating social costs and benefits of all affected parties.

cost code
A numbering system used to describe the type, source and purpose of all costs and income.

cost of capital
The annual percentage cost of a particular source of capital. See also weighted average cost of capital.

current cost accounting
A procedure for adjusting items in a company profit and loss account and balance sheet for the effects of inflation.

decision tree
A diagram depicting alternative courses of action as branches of a tree.

depreciation
A proportion of the original or current replacement cost of a fixed asset which is charged as an expense in a company profit and loss account.

discounted cash flow (DCF) yield
A measure of the true rate of profitability expected on a project. It represents the maximum rate of interest which could be paid on the diminishing capital balance of an investment.

dividend growth model
A method of valuing the cost of equity capital, combining the expected dividend yield and the growth rate of dividends.

dividend yield
The dividend per share expressed as a percentage of the current market price of the share.

earnings
The profit attributable to the ordinary shareholders after interest, tax and any preference dividends have been deducted, irrespective of whether that profit is distributed or retained in the company.

earnings per share
Earnings for the year divided by the number of ordinary shares issued.

earnings yield
The earnings per ordinary share expressed as a percentage of the current market price of the share.

equity
See shareholders' funds.

fixed assets
Land and buildings, plant and machinery, vehicles, furniture and office equipment used by the firm itself and not for resale to customers.

gearing
The relationship of borrowed capital to owners' capital or borrowed capital to total capital employed.

historic cost
The actual cost incurred at the time of purchase irrespective of the item's current value.

income tax
The tax levied on the income of employees and on profits of self-employed persons.

inflation accounting
See current cost accounting.

internal rate of return (IRR)
See DCF yield.

investment appraisal
The use of accounting and statistical techniques to determine the worthwhileness of new investment projects.

leverage
See gearing.

life cycle cost
The total cost of owning and using a physical asset over its whole life, from its original design and manufacture to its eventual disposal.

mainstream tax
The balance of the corporation tax liability after the advance payments have been made.

mutually exclusive
Projects are said to be mutually exclusive when they compete against each other and only one alternative may be chosen.

net cash flow
A comparison of total cash in with total cash out for each year, being part of an investment appraisal.

net present value (NPV)
The total of all positive and negative cash flows on a project after they have been expressed in present value terms. A project is said to be viable when a positive net present value results from discounting at the company's required rate of return.

nominal return
The apparent rate of return on an investment calculated from inflated future cash flows.

opportunity cost
The value foregone from the next best use of the same resources.

payback
The number of years taken to recover the original sum invested.

portfolio theory
A branch of investment appraisal concerned with risk and rewards. It particularly refers to the effect of adding one new investment to an existing portfolio.

present value
The equivalent value now of a sum of money receivable in a later year.

probability factor
The likelihood of occurrence of a particular event represented by a number of ranging from 0 to 1.0. A probability factor of 0 implies no chance of the event occurring whilst a factor of 1.0 depicts the certainty of it happening.

profit and loss account
A statement of trading performance relating the sales income to the cost of sales and overheads for the same period.

profitability index
A means of ranking investments in order of attractiveness when appraised by the net present value method. The index number is calculated by dividing the net present value of inflows by the net present value of the initial outflow.

rate of return
A somewhat arbitrary method of investment appraisal which relates the average annual profit to the average capital invested in the project.

real return
The nominal rate of return on an investment less the rate of inflation.

rights issue
An invitation to existing shareholders to subscribe for new shares when a company requires further capital.

risk premium
The rate by which the basic cost of capital is increased to allow for the expected risk on an investment.

sensitivity analysis
A process to discover the responsiveness of the profitability of an investment to variations in individual items making up the cash flows.

shadow price
An imputed value used in CBA for services or commodities with no market price.

shareholders' funds
The total amount of shareholders' investment in the company comprising both issued share capital, retained profits and other reserves. It is also equal to the value of all the company's assets after deducting all debts owing to outside parties.

sunk cost
A cost which was previously incurred and is now irrelevant to the decision under review, other than any opportunity cost it may possess.

terotechnology
A combination of management, financial, engineering and other practices applied to physical assets in pursuit of economic life cycle costs.

weighted average cost of capital
The overall cost of capital for a firm calculated from a weighted average of the individual costs of each source of capital.

working capital
That part of a firm's total capital which is tied up in stocks, work-in-progress and granting credit to customers. It is equal to the total value of all stocks, customers' debts and cash less the amount owing to suppliers.

Appendix 5

Microcomputer program to calculate NPV and DCF yield

The program enables the user to establish quickly DCF yield and NPV values for a project. Sensitivity analysis can be rapidly carried out by changing cash flow values and observing the effects.

The program is written in basic BASIC so there should be little or no difficulty in using it with any micro. No printer output is available with the program as given. The user may add appropriate lines of program to suit his/her particular machine.

Method of use

Inputs: The user is asked to specify the life of the project in number of years. The user then inputs the net cash flows, positive or negative, for each year from Year 0 onwards.

Options: Having inputted the basic cash flow data the user then has options to:

1. Obtain the DCF yield (internal rate of return).
2. Derive the NPV for any choice of discounting rate.
3. Change the cash flow value for any existing year.
4. Add cash flows for additional years.
5. Delete cash flows.

Output: The program gives outputs to VDU screen as follows:

1. Menu of options.
2. DCF yield to a precision of 0.01 per cent.

3 NPV display, showing for each year the year number, cash flow, discounting factor and present value.

Program listing

```
100 REM DCF/NPV PROGRAM – BY BRIAN DAY – 1986
110 CLS:REM CLEAR SCREEN
120 INPUT"NO OF YEARS";Y:Z=Y+5
130 DIM C(Z):REM PROVISION FOR 5 EXTRA YEARS
140 FOR J = 0 TO Y
150 PRINT"YEAR";J;:INPUT"CASH FLOW";C(J)
160 NEXT J
1000 REM OPTIONS ***********************************
1005 PRINT
1010 PRINT"D = DCF, N = NPV, C = CHANGE DATA, R =
     RUN, X = EXIT"
1020 INPUT"ENTER OPTION AND PRESS RETURN";A$
1030 IF A$ = "D" THEN 2000
1040 IF A$ = "N" THEN 3000
1050 IF A$ = "C" THEN 4000
1060 IF A$ = "X" THEN END
1070 IF A$ = "R" THEN RUN
1080 GOTO 1000
2000 REM DCF ALGORITHM *****************************
2010 P=.01:HR=512:LR=-128:PR=0
2020 R=(HR + LR)/2
2025 IF ABS(PR - R) < P THEN R=INT(R*100+.5)/100:
     GOTO 2080
2030 GOSUB 5000
2040 IF NP > 0 THEN LR = R:GOTO 2060
2050 HR = R
2060 PR = R
2070 GOTO 2020
2080 PRINT:PRINT"DCF RATE OF RETURN";R;"%"
2090 GOTO 1000
3000 REM NPV ALGORITHM *****************************
3010 PRINT:INPUT"DISCOUNTING RATE";R
3020 PRINT"YEAR","CASH FLOW","FACTOR", "PRESENT
     VALUE"
```

```
3030 PRINT
3040 GOSUB 5000
3050 PRINT,,,"NPV";INT(NP*10+.5)/10
3060 GOTO 1000
4000 REM CHANGE DATA ******************************
4010 PRINT:INPUT"CHANGE WHICH YEAR";CY
4015 IF CY > Z THEN PRINT"ERROR":GOTO 4010
4020 PRINT"PRESENT VALUE";C(CY);:INPUT"NEW VALUE"
     ;C(CY)
4030 FOR J = 0 TO Z
4040 IF C(J) <> 0 THEN Y = J
4050 NEXT J
4070 GOTO 1000
5000 REM DISCOUNTING ROUTINE *********************
5010 NP=0:FOR J = 0 TO Y
5020 DF=1/(1+R/100)^J:PV = C(J)*DF
5030 NP=NP+PV:DF=INT(DF*10000+.5)/10000
5035 PV=INT(PV*10000+.5)/10000
5040 IF A$ = "N" THEN PRINT J,C(J),DF,PV
5050 NEXT J
5060 RETURN
```

Appendix 6
Examination questions

Question 1

A company is at present using the payback method in the appraisal of investment projects. The following information is available regarding four projects which are currently being analysed:

	Project 1 £	Project 2 £	Project 3 £	Project 4 £
Annual P/L a/c items:				
Sales	90,000	250,000	100,000	120,000
Direct costs	30,000	170,000	55,000	70,000
Allocation of H.O. costs	9,000	25,000	10,000	12,000
Depreciation	20,000	40,000	25,000	40,000
Interest	24,000	20,000	10,000	8,000
Capital cost of project	240,000	200,000	100,000	80,000
Life of project	12 years	5 years	4 years	2 years

The chief accountant has recommended that the accounting rate of return method should be adopted instead of payback. However, a management consultant who has been called in to advise on corporate planning procedures has argued in favour of the use of discounted cash flow methods; he has suggested that either the net present value or the internal rate of return approach should be utilised. He estimates that the company's cost of capital is 20 per cent.

Required:

(*a*) Calculate the relative attractiveness of each project under:

(*i*) the payback method
(*ii*) the accounting rate of return method;
(*iii*) the net present value method; and
(*iv*) the internal rate of return method

(*b*) Explain how the cost of capital of a company should be calculated.

(*c*) Consider the impact of a change in the capital structure of a company upon its cost of capital.

(ICSA Business Finance, June 1983)

Question 2

Mozart plc is considering at 31 December 1985 the introduction of a new model, the Idomeneo, to its range of bicycles. This would involve the following expenditure and receipts on the part of the company:

(*a*) An extension to the company's factory which would cost £200,000. This would involve the demolition of storage facilities which had a written down value of £20,000 and a replacement cost of £40,000. These facilities have not been used for some months, and the company had intended to sell them for £35,000. At the end of 5 years the new extension could be used for storage purposes and rented out for £5,000 per annum.

(*b*) The Idomeneo is expected to have a market life of 5 years and the market research team has provided the following forecasts regarding the level of demand at various selling prices:

	No. units sold per annum		
	1986	*1987*	*1988-90*
£90	3,600	3,800	4,000
£95	3,000	3,300	3,500
£100	2,400	2,600	3,000

(*c*) The parts to be used for making the bicycle are as follows:

(*i*) Wheels. The company has a stock of 6,000 sets of special wheels which it bought two years ago at £10 per set for a bicycle which has been discontinued. These wheels cannot be used in any other way by the company if the Idomeneo project does not go ahead. Their scrap value is £2 per set and their current replacement cost is £15 per set.

(*ii*) Frame. The company has 2,000 of these in stock. They cost £40, have a scrap value of £10, and the current replacement cost is £45. These frames can be used for other bicycles which the company makes.

(*d*) The labour costs are £10 per unit. By launching the Idomeneo the company will be able to continue to employ 20 workers who would otherwise have been made redundant at a cost of £1,000 each.

(*e*) The marketing budget will need to be increased by £10,000 per annum to promote the new bicycle. The company accountant argues that there should be an allocation of existing marketing expenditure as well and that each unit should bear a charge of £10 for marketing.

(*f*) General overheads will increase by £6,000 per annum due to the expansion. The accountant proposes to make an overhead charge of £12 per unit.

(*g*) The machinery needed for production purposes can be transferred from another production line. It has a written-down value of £40,000 and scrap value of £10,000, and is depreciated at £8,000 per annum. A replacement machine for the other production line will cost £30,000.

The company's cost of capital is 20 per cent.

You are required to advise the directors of the company whether the expansion should be undertaken and at what price the bicycle should be sold. Your report should explain how sensitivity analysis might be applied in appraising the project.

Ignore inflation and taxation.

(ICSA Business Finance, June 1985)

Question 3

A company has the following share capital and long-term liabilities in its balance sheet:

		£
Share capital and reserves:		
Ordinary shares of 25p		1,000,000
10% Preference shares of £1		500,000
Revaluation reserve		800,000
Retained earnings		1,200,000
		3,500,000
Debentures		
6% Debentures 1982-1986	2,000,000	
10% Debentures 1995-2000	1,500,000	
		3,500,000
		7,000,000

The market value of these securities is as follows:

Ordinary shares	500p
Preference shares	80p
6% debentures	90p
10% debentures	80p

The current earnings per ordinary share are 100p and these are expected to continue for the foreseeable future.

The company is contemplating a new project costing £4,700,000 which is rather more risky than those currently undertaken by the company. As a result shareholders would require their return to be increased by one-tenth if it were undertaken. The project may be financed in any of the following ways:

(*i*) The issue of one million ordinary shares to an insurance company at 470 p each.

(*ii*) A rights issue of two million new shares at 235p each.

(*iii*) The issue of £5,000,000 12 per cent debentures at a price of £94. This would increase the financial risk of the company to a point where the ordinary shareholders would expect their return to be increased by a further one-tenth.

You are required:

(*a*) To calculate the capital gearing of the company before the issue.

(*b*) To calculate the minimum amount of annual profit which the project must generate if it is to be acceptable under each of the above alternatives.

(*c*) To define and explain the following terms:

cost of equity capital
weighted average cost of capital
marginal cost of capital.

Ignore taxation.

(ICSA Business Finance, June 1985)

Question 4

Cost of capital is an elusive yet important concept of financial management.

One theory argues that the cost of equity capital is the discount rate required to reduce an infinite stream of future dividends to the present share price:

Required:

(*a*) What cost of equity capital is implied in the following information?

Share price £2.00 ex. div.
Dividend recently paid 20p per share
Dividend growth expected 10 per cent per annum
Dividends paid annually

(*b*) What will be the effect of the company undertaking projects yielding a return in excess of the cost of capital determined in (*a*)?

(*c*) How can the company reduce the cost of equity capital?

(Certified Diploma)

Question 5

Rapid Growth plc has been analysing a series of perpetual projects which are available for immediate investment. The internal rates of return offered by these projects are as follows:

Project	Cost £'000s	Rate of return (%)
1	200	25
2	400	23
3	300	20
4	300	19
5	500	17
6	1,700	16
7	1,400	15

The company has £1,000,000 available for investment and its capital structure is as follows:

	£
Share capital (ordinary shares of 50p)	5,000,000
Reserves	16,000,000
9% debentures (irredeemable)	10,000,000
	31,000,000

The ordinary shares have a market value of 150p each and the debentures stand in the market at £75 per £100 nominal value. The current earnings per share, which are not expected to vary in the future, are 31.5p.

You are informed that projects 1 and 2 are mutually exclusive and that projects 4 and 5 are also mutually exclusive.

Required:

(*i*) Explain which projects should be accepted on the basis of the above information.

(*ii*) Explain how your answer would be affected if the company could raise an additional £3,000,000 by the issue of debentures at 12 per cent. Such an issue would increase by one-tenth the rate of return required by the ordinary shareholders.

(Ignore taxation)

(ICSA Business Finance, Dec. 1985)

Question 6

A local government department is proposing to purchase a mechanical hedge-cutting machine to replace existing manual work. Manpower savings are greatest when using a machine with the largest cutting blade but the initial purchase cost increases more than proportionately to the width of the cut achieved.

The relevant cost details are:

Cutter size	12"	18"	24"	30"	36"
	£000	£000	£000	£000	£000
Purchase cost	20	30	45	70	100
Annual operating cost savings after deduction of depreciation	8	10	11	8	6

Depreciation — straight-line method over ten years
Taxation — assume no tax allowances or tax payments.

The local council will not authorise any proposed investment which does not yield a discounted cash flow (DCF) return of 15 per cent per annum. All proposals meeting this target are further subject to an overall total investment limit.

You are required to:

(*a*) calculate the discounted cash flow (DCF) yield for each of the five machines;

(*b*) state the largest size machine which could be purchased and meet the 15 per cent investment criterion;

(*c*) list five factors that would influence the decision on this particular investment if there are more investment projects than funds available; at least two should be in favour of proceeding with it and at least two supporting deferment.

(CIMA Management Accounting, May 1985)

Question 7

Kirkby plc does not have any overseas projects but appraises all its UK projects by utilising both accounting rate of return and payback. Kirkby's management explain their preference for the two appraisal methods used by stating 'accounting rate of return, based on average profit to initial investment, will indicate how each project will be reflected in the published accounts and will show its impact on our "profit to capital employed" ratio; we do not undertake projects which will reduce this ratio. Payback indicates how long our money is at risk by determining the length of time it takes for the initial investment in the project to be repaid by the total of accounting profit plus depreciation.'

Both methods are applied on a pre-tax basis as Kirkby's management argue, 'A pre- and post-tax analysis differs only by the effect of the tax rate and this is outside the control of management. Hence tax should be excluded for practical project appraisal.'

Kirkby is subject to tax at a rate of 50 per cent with a delay of one year. Kirkby has erratic profit levels and these are frequently insufficient to enable it to utilise in full all first-year allowances at the earliest opportunity.

A recent small project appraised by Kirkby was the purchase of industrial equipment, eligible for 100 per cent first-year allowances, costing £90,000 which was expected to produce the following results:

	Per year (£'000s)	*Years 1 to 3 (£'000s)*
Sales		100
Incremental cash costs	50	
Depreciation	30	80
Annual profit		20

The life of the profit is 3 years and no salvage value is expected. Receipts from sales are 20 per cent in year of sale and 80 per cent in the following year. Cash costs arise in the year to which they relate.

Required:

Using the project whose details are given above as an example, if required, advise Kirkby of the practical and theoretical deficiencies of:

(*a*) its current appraisal techniques, and
(*b*) appraising projects on a pre-, rather than post-, tax basis.

(CACA Financial Management, Dec. 1984)

Question 8

For the last four years Faversham plc has been pursuing an expansion programme which it has finance by both retained earnings and large amounts of externally raised debt finance. The expansion programme has the same risk characteristics as Faversham's previous activities and will therefore not alter the risk of Faversham's operating activities.

As part of the final stages of the expansion programme the management team of Faversham is currently considering raising an additional loan to finance a further new factory. Although the proposed investment in the factory is expected to yield about 1.5-2 per cent below the return normally expected from such an investment and the only loan obtainable is costly at 3 per cent above the current market rate for corporate debt, it is felt that both the loan and the investment are justified as the expected return on the investment is about 4 per cent higher than the cost of the loan (all figures are after considering tax consequences). Faversham therefore intends to obtain the loan and to invest in the factory.

Required:

(*a*) Write a concise report to the management of Faversham which

(*i*) explains, without reference to Faversham's specific circumstances, the impact of debt finance on both the weighted average cost of capital and total firm valuation, both with and without corporate taxation, and

(*ii*) comments specifically on, and explains the importance of, all the issues implied by the particular circumstances surrounding Faversham's current proposal which should be considered before reaching a decision on the desirability of undertaking the current loan and investment.

(*b*) Briefly outline the major factors to be considered by management when deciding on the amount of debt to be utilised in a firm's capital structure in practice.

(CACA Financial Management, June 1985)

Question 9

A company is considering investing in a new manufacturing facility with the following characteristics:

A initial investment £350,000 – scrap value nil;
B expected life 10 years;
C sales volume 20,000 units per year;
D selling price £20 per unit
E variable direct costs £15 per unit;
F fixed costs excluding depreciation £25,000 per year.

The project shows an internal rate of return (IRR) of 17 per cent. The managing director is concerned about the viability of the investment as the return is close to the company's hurdle rate of 15 per cent. He has requested a sensitivity analysis.

You are required to:

(*a*) recalculate the internal rate of return (IRR) assuming each of the characteristics A to F above, in isolation, varies adversely by 10 per cent.
(*b*) advise the managing director of the most vulnerable area likely to prevent the project meeting the company's hurdle rate;
(*c*) explain what further work might be undertaken to improve the value of the sensitivity analysis undertaken in (*a*);
(*d*) re-evaluate the situation if another company, already manufacturing a similar product, offered to supply the units at £18 each – this would reduce the investment required to £25,000 and the fixed costs to £10,000.

(CIMA Management Accounting, May 1986)

Question 10

It is commonly accepted that a crucial factor in the financial decisions of a company, including the evaluation of capital investment proposals, is the cost of capital.

You are required to:

(*a*) explain in simple terms what is meant by the 'cost of equity capital' for a particular company;

(*b*) calculate the cost of equity capital for X plc from the data given below, using two alternative methods, i.e.:

(*i*) a dividend growth model
(*ii*) the capital asset pricing model;

Data

X plc:	Current price per share on Stock Exchange	£1.20
	Current annual gross dividend per share	£0.10
	Expected average annual growth rate of dividends	7%
	Beta coefficient for X plc shares	0.5
Expected rate of return on risk-free securities		8%
Expected return on the market portfolio		12%

(*c*) state, for each model separately, the main simplifying assumptions made and express your opinion whether, in view of these assumptions, the models yield results that can be used safely in practice.

(CIMA Financial Management, May 1986)

Index